Top
Telemarketing
Techniques

Top Telemarketing Techniques

Ellen Bendremer

CAREER
PRESS

THE CAREER PRESS, INC.
Franklin Lakes, NJ

TOP TELEMARKETING TECHNIQUES
EDITED BY JODI BRANDON
TYPESET BY STACEY A. FARKAS
Cover design by Mada Design, Inc. / NYC
Printed in the U.S.A. by Book-mart Press

To order this title, please call toll-free 1-800-CAREER-1 (NJ and Canada: 201-848-0310) to order using VISA or MasterCard, or for further information on books from Career Press.

The Career Press, Inc., 3 Tice Road, PO Box 687,
Franklin Lakes, NJ 07417
www.careerpress.com

Library of Congress Cataloging-in-Publication Data
Bendremer, Ellen.
    Top telemarketing techniques / by Ellen Bendremer
        p. cm.
    Includes index.
    ISBN 1-56414-685-5 (paper)
        1. Telemarketing. 2. Telephone selling. 3. Sales personnel—Training of. I. Title.

HF5415.1265.B463 2003
658.8'4—dc21   2003043455

I dedicate this book to my husband, Sandy, who makes me laugh, comforts me, encourages me, and uncompromisingly demonstrates his love for me; and to my daughter Emily, the sunshine of my life, who continually reminds me of what's important and makes every day so special. Watching her laugh, learn, and grow each day continues to be the most rewarding and exciting experience of my life.

ACKNOWLEDGMENTS

I wish to express my heartfelt thanks to the following people for their endless encouragement, love, and support:

Arthur Bromfield, my father, friend, and confidant. He has helped me in countless ways to shape my life and achieve success in my career. I am grateful for all of his love and confidence, and for always believing in me.

Ken, Yukari, Evan, and Jessica Bromfield; Wendy and Mark Rapaport; Michelle, Dave, and Elise Andelman; Sy and Phyllis Bendremer; Linda Bromfield; Rick Bendremer; Jeff, Ellie, and Sol Bendremer; Danielle Wozniak; as well as my dearest friends, Mark Giordani and Jason Rich, who prove over and over again that the limits of friendship are boundless.

Contents

Chapter 1

SALES ARE JUST A PHONE CALL AWAY

For the past 15 years, I have made a successful living as a telemarketing and sales professional—and you can, too! There are countless products and services you can sell over the telephone. There is also a wide range of telesales techniques you can use to successfully convey your sales message. Once you have acquired the knowledge and have developed the skills necessary to sell products/services using the telephone, your potential as a telesales professional is truly limitless.

Over the years, I have worked within large call centers; developed telemarketing campaigns for large, medium, and small businesses; and I have done consulting for a wide range of companies. Using the telephone as my primary sales tool, I have discovered strategies and secrets that have allowed me to sell more than $10 million worth of products and services to individuals and businesses, almost always without leaving my own office.

One of the great things about telemarketing is that it can be done from anywhere. In fact, millions of the dollars I have generated in sales thus far in my career have been from my home office, which gives me the ability to earn the income I desire yet have the flexible daily schedule I enjoy. Telemarketing is more than a job for me. It's become my passion! I can only begin to describe the excitement and sense of accomplishment I feel as I constantly make contact with new prospects using the telephone and ultimately close sale after sale. There is great satisfaction in knowing that I have sold a product or service that will benefit the customer, while, at the same time, I have generated revenues for my company (or my client) and have earned a sales commission for myself.

For me, telemarketing is fun! It's also challenging and highly rewarding. Whether you're planning to become a full-time telesales professional or you hope to develop telemarketing skills that can be incorporated into your current, more traditional in-person sales efforts, *Top Telemarketing Techniques* shares much of the knowledge I have painstakingly acquired over the years and offers you the information you need to begin achieving success almost immediately. In addition to learning from my experiences, by reading this book, you'll also learn from the experiences of other highly successful telesales professionals. Thus, you can learn from our mistakes without making them yourself and begin to master the techniques that work best in a wide range of situations.

Whether you're new to telemarketing or a seasoned professional looking to improve your skills, this book will take you step by step through many of the common obstacles and challenges faced by all telemarketers, including:

- Developing your customized prospect list.
- Creating effective telemarketing scripts.
- Developing the right attitude.
- Overcoming objections.
- Coping with rejection.
- Getting through to the right decision-makers.

- ♦ Dramatically improving your closing techniques.
- ♦ Utilizing software and tools to maximize your sales.

Although nothing can replace the need for you to acquire firsthand experience, if you begin your telemarketing efforts equipped with the right knowledge and strategies, your chances for success increase exponentially. Sure, telemarketing can be challenging and time-consuming, but, with practice, you'll learn to enjoy acquiring the skills and experience you need to close sale after sale using the telephone!

I invite you to read this book in its entirety, then to go back and review each section of the book as you begin to plan and ultimately to implement your own telemarketing efforts. Virtually all of the information you'll need will be found within this book, however, additional resources are also available from my Website (*www.EllenBendremer.com*). No matter what you sell, you'll soon discover that the telephone is an extremely powerful tool for finding and qualifying leads and closing sales.

My greatest hope is that you, too, will soon learn to appreciate the power of telemarketing and discover how to reap the incredible benefits of using the telephone as your primary sales tool.

Let's Get Started!

Depending on your perspective, the word *telemarketing* can conjure up very different images. As a business owner selling to consumers or other businesses, telemarketing may be a solution for vastly improving sales, generating greater success, and greatly expanding the reach of your business without ever leaving the comfort of your office. If you're a consumer sitting at home trying to relax when the phone rings at the most inopportune time, that same word can conjure up feelings of annoyance, frustration, or fear of being caught up in some type of scam.

The *Merriam-Webster Dictionary* defines telemarketing as the marketing of goods or services by telephone. It's a word that was added to the dictionary back in 1980, when it became obvious that the telephone was changing the way companies did business.

In general, people are busy. They don't want to be bothered by others trying to sell them products or services that aren't needed. A successful telemarketer can quickly capture the attention of the person he or she is calling and prove to that person that what you're offering could be beneficial. With the right knowledge and skills, as a telesales professional, you can quickly break down the psychological barriers many people have developed against telemarketers and close sales.

The Telemarketing Industry

The ongoing growth in the telemarketing field is staggering. Finding timely and accurate statistics relating to this field and the use of the telephone to make sales is difficult, but the following are some statistics that will give you an idea of how many people are involved in this industry and how many sales are done over the telephone on an annual basis:

- "More than 70% of business transactions take place over the telephone." (Source: GeoTel, citing Gartner Group, September 1998.)
- "Outbound telemarketing reached a record $482.2 billion in sales in 1998, including $209.5 billion in sales to consumers." (Source: Direct Marketing Association, January 1999, *U.S. Direct Marketing Today: Economic Impact*, 1998.)
- "Nearly 265,000 U.S. companies will be using telemarketing in the near future." (Source: CallOmni Telemarketing.)

+ "The overall consumer penetration of business-to-consumer telemarketing adds up to more than 47.5 million households." (Source: CallOmni Telemarketing.)

+ "$700 billion in products and services were sold through call centers in 1997 and this figure is expanding by 20% annually." (Source: GeoTel citing *Telemarketing Magazine*, September 1998.)

+ "There are approximately 7,000,000 agents now working in 70,000 call centers in the [United States], with an annual growth rate of up to 20% in agent positions." (Source: Davox, citing F.A.C./ Equities, 1998.)

+ "The worldwide call center services market totaled $23 billion in revenues in 1998, and is projected to double to $58.6 billion by 2003. (This is based on dividing the overall call center service marketing into these segments: consulting, systems integration, and outsourcing.) Outsourcing is the largest segment, with $17 billion in 1998, or 74% of the total market, headed for $42 billion in 2003." (Source: IDC, June 1999.)

Should You Be Reading This Book?

Telemarketing is a vast field used in many ways by companies of all sizes and in all industries. Thus, anyone with an interest in better utilizing the telephone within his or her business, or who wants to learn the skills needed to be a (more successful) telemarketer, will greatly benefit from this book.

This book was written for the following types of people:

+ People interested in breaking into the telemarketing field.

- Current telemarketers and telesales professionals looking to improve their telephone sales skills and generate even greater results from their efforts.
- Traditional salespeople looking to use the telephone as a powerful sales tool capable of saving them time, resources, and money.
- Sales managers or call center supervisors who work with or manage teams of telemarketers.
- Business owners looking to expand their business and reach a larger customer base.

What You'll Learn From This Book

Top Telemarketing Techniques is all about using the telephone to enhance sales, fostering better relationships with customers, and how to make it easier to target prospects. Much of what you'll be reading within this book focuses on building the skills you need to become a top-notch telemarketer or telesales professional, whether you're engaged in inbound or outbound telemarketing. Depending on what type of business you're in and what your job responsibilities entail, how you use the telephone will vary. However, if you are or will be using the telephone in any part of your sales, marketing, or customer service efforts, many of the skills needed to do this successfully are the same.

As you're about to learn, many skills need to be combined in order to be a successful telemarketer. In addition to being able to sell a product/service, you need to be able to:

- Communicate effectively using your voice.
- Interact extremely well with total strangers and foster relationships and trust quickly.
- Overcome objections; have the ability to negotiate and/or resolve conflict.

- Be highly organized and be able to manage your time.
- Stay motivated and be able to motivate your prospects.
- Understand and utilize a knowledge about your prospects in terms of their needs and desires.
- Follow the guidelines or procedures dictated by your employer.

To achieve success as a telemarketer, you'll need to invest the necessary time and effort to learn and master a variety of different skills. Only then will you be able to truly tap your potential for generating the sales results you and your employer want. This book divides up the skills you need, explains them in detail, and then offers strategies for developing and utilizing them. Once you develop a basic understanding of each skill involved in the telemarketing process, however, it's up to you to practice and hone those skills and discover how to properly incorporate them into the telesales work you are or will be doing. If you're already engaged in telemarketing, *Top Telemarketing Techniques* will offer you proven strategies for enhancing your skills in order to generate even greater results.

Your Voice + Telephone = Sales

As a salesperson, you could take your product/service on the road, visit one prospect at a time, and engage in an in-person meeting with each prospect. Although this sales method is highly effective, it's also time-consuming and costly. Another alternative is to advertise or engage in traditional marketing activities so your prospects and potential customers come to you. This, too, can be a highly effective, but costly, endeavor, although, it's always nice to run a targeted ad and have prequalified prospects knocking at your door or calling you on the phone.

In the time it takes you to make just one in-person sales call, you could stay at your office, pick up the telephone, and potentially reach dozens, if not hundreds, of potential prospects, using basic outbound telemarketing efforts. Likewise, for far less than the cost of running a print, radio, or television ad (that reaches a general audience as opposed to a targeted audience made up of people or companies that need or want your product/service), you could call hundreds of prequalified prospects and personally introduce them to your company's products or services using the telephone.

Using your voice as a sales tool, the telephone, and perhaps some related technology, you can cost effectively launch a telemarketing effort that will allow your company to increase its sales, reach more qualified prospects faster, and more easily reach its sales goals. At the same time you're working to expand your customer base, the telephone can be used to enhance and strengthen the relationships you have with existing customers and help you generate more repeat business.

By learning how to "dial for dollars," you can transform the telephone that's already sitting on your desk into a virtual money-making machine with unlimited potential.

Throughout this book, the terms *telemarketing* and *telesales* are used interchangeably. However, some people define telemarketing as the use of the telephone to make contact with prospects, whereas telesales involves actually moving the prospect further down the sales cycle or sales pipeline. The skills required of a telemarketer and/or telesales professional, as you'll soon see, are identical.

Why You Need To Read This Book

Whether you're a seasoned salesperson or someone first entering the field, there are many different strategies you can use to achieve success using the telephone as your primary sales tool. You could spend months or years discovering and developing the strategies that work best for your product/service, or you could learn from seasoned experts and utilize the knowledge and secrets they've already discovered, starting immediately—and that's what *Top Telemarketing Techniques* has to offer.

Due to a variety of factors, more and more companies are being forced to continuously cut costs, boost productivity, and struggle for success. Although their mandate might be to improve sales, the resources available to do this are being cut. For companies in this situation, the telephone can become a useful tool.

For individuals, a career as a telemarketer can be long-lasting and highly lucrative, especially once you perfect your skills, gain experience, and develop a track record. After that, as long as you truly believe in the product/service you're selling, you will be able to sell almost anything over the telephone. It's important to understand, however, that not everyone is cut out to be a successful telemarketer or even a salesperson. If you wind up in a job that you're not suited for, within a year you could get burned out and see a drastic reduction in your productivity because you're unhappy. The employee turnover rate relating to telemarketing jobs (particularly in entry-level positions) is extremely high. Back in 1999, Purdue University Center for Customer Driven Quality issued a report stating, "Inbound centers have an average annual turnover of 26% for full-time reps, and 33% for part-timers. Nearly half of centers said that part-timers handle 5% or less of their total calls." To avoid landing in a job you won't succeed in, the first step is to insure that in addition to having the skills necessary to be a successful telemarketer, you also have the personality, internal drive, and mindset needed.

Chapter 3 focuses on various types of telemarketing and telesales jobs and how to pursue a career in this field. From this chapter, you'll discover what skills and personality traits a typical telemarketing or telesales job requires, what the job responsibilities include, and what types of people typically excel in this type of career. Even after reading this book, if you're not sure you have what it takes to enter into this field, you might consider participating in a behavior, attitude, and soft-skill assessment to help make your career decision. A test such as this is a great tool that could help you determine if you're suitable for this type of job.

Obviously, no assessment test will offer 100-percent conclusive results, but many individuals use this type of test to help them determine a suitable career path. Employers use it to hire the applicants most suited for a job by taking into account more than actual skills.

Defining Your Needs and Goals

Before continuing on, it's important to define your needs and goals. For an individual looking to get into the telemarketing field or enhance your skills, your goals might be:

- To learn the skills required to become a successful telemarketer or telesales professional.
- To perfect or hone your sales skills and discover strategies for using the telephone to reach more prospects, make more sales, and improve your relationships with existing customers.
- To discover and incorporate new strategies for improving your closing ratio.
- To expand your client base and tap new markets.
- To determine how to deal with all of your prospects' objections and transform rejection into sales.

There are many reasons why a company of any size and in almost any industry would want to explore how telemarketing could be used to benefit their business. Before a company incorporates an in-house sales team and kicks off a telemarketing effort, it must develop a thorough understanding of who its target customer is and how the telephone can be used to better communicate with that customer.

According to Tom Morrill, president and CEO of North Andover, Massachusetts–based Actegy, a sales consulting company, "It's critical that any company, no matter what its size, first clearly understands their value proposition in the marketplace. Who are you selling to? What problems are you solving and how? With these answers in mind, you need to clearly understand the client's buying behavior. Once you understand their buying behavior, you can comfortably determine whether or not you should be using inside sales, outside sales, or some form of channel model. The companies that have been most successful determine when and how to properly allocate their telemarketing and telesales resources into the customer's buying cycle."

When a customer does not require face-to-face time during the sales cycle, it's an excellent indication that utilizing a telemarketing approach is viable. "For our clients, we follow some carefully defined steps to better understand their client's buying behavior before we attempt to implement any types of telemarketing sales strategies. We determine, on behalf of our clients, what their customers require during their purchase cycle," adds Morrill, who believes that whether or not a company can successfully use telemarketing as a sales tool is dictated by who the customer is and what his or her buying habits are.

Why Companies Use Telemarketing

In the next few chapters, you'll learn some of the ways companies are successfully using telemarketing strategies to:

- Find new customers.
- Reduce the costs of sales.
- Expand the reach of their business.
- Build better relationships with existing customers.
- Improve customer service and/or technical support.
- Handle incoming orders and process information requests.

Any time a company chooses to utilize telemarketing, to achieve success it must rely on a team of telemarketers or telesales professionals who have the knowledge, skills, and experience to effectively sell and communicate with prospects and customers using the telephone. Based on the needs of a company, an individual telemarketer's responsibilities will vary greatly, so it's important that the right people, with the right skills, be used. *Top Telemarketing Techniques* will help companies define their needs and assist people in perfecting their telemarketing skills to properly fulfill those needs.

In the next chapter, you'll learn more about telemarketing and how it's used by companies. Chapter 3 focuses on various job opportunities and career paths someone interested in this field can pursue. The rest of this book focuses on developing the right skills and knowledge needed to become a successful telemarketer and will walk you through the entire process of selling your product/service using the telephone as your primary sales tool.

Chapter 2

THE POWER
OF TELESALES

On March 10, 1876, in Boston, Massachusetts, Alexander Graham Bell invented the telephone. At the time, who would have guessed that this tool would not only revolutionize how people communicate, but also how business would be conducted throughout the world? Today, millions of people rely on the telephone as their primary business tool, whether it's for making sales, handling customer service or technical support, gathering information, or simply communicating with customers.

This chapter focuses on several ways you can begin better utilizing the telephone in your business, whether you're a business leader, telesales professional, customer service representative, or small business owner.

Why Utilize Telemarketing?

In business, there are only a handful of ways to contact and sell to customers and clients:

- ◆ You can convince them to visit your office or retail store.

- You can sell your products/services via a Website (e-commerce).
- You can send (mail, fax, or e-mail) catalogs and sales brochures.
- You can visit the potential customer, making in-person sales calls.
- You can call the prospect on the telephone.

With the possible exception of walk-in traffic to your office or store, one of the easiest and least expensive ways to reach prospects and potential customers is via the telephone. From the comfort of your office (or home office), you can call dozens, perhaps hundreds, of prospects per day at a minimal cost.

The time and financial cost of sending out unsolicited catalogs and sales brochures can be tremendous, yet an even greater cost is incurred when making in-person sales calls to prospects and current customers. For example, making an in-person sales call involves getting in your car, driving to the prospect's home or office, visiting that prospect, and hoping the appropriate decision-maker is available. Then, you must wait for the person to meet with you, do your sales pitch, get back in your car, and begin the whole process again with the next prospect. In some cases, you may even need to take an airplane, rent a car, and plan an overnight stay at a hotel just to meet with a single prospect or client. During that time, you could have made many calls, to many prospects, instead of spending your time focusing on a single in-person sales call.

Using the telephone, not only will you save a tremendous amount of time, but your cost of sale will drop dramatically as you vastly improve your sales ratio (the number of sales you close versus the number of sales pitches you make). From the seller's standpoint, telemarketing certainly makes sense in many sales situations; in addition, from the customer's perspective, it's also a time saver. After all, it's a lot easier for a busy person to allocate a few minutes for a telephone call than it is to block out time in his or her schedule for a time-consuming in-person meeting/sales presentation.

Thus, if you're selling any type of product or service that can be sold using the telephone as your primary sales tool, telemarketing (outbound calling) certainly makes a lot of sense. Likewise, if your product/service requires an in-person sales meeting, because it needs to be seen or experienced firsthand by the prospect, the telephone can be a valuable tool for pre-qualifying prospects and scheduling those in-person sales meetings. You'll soon discover that just about any business can greatly benefit from outbound telemarketing in order to boost sales and/or reduce the cost associated with making sales.

The Pros and Cons of Telemarketing

From the seller's standpoint, the pros of telemarketing are numerous. As you already know, you can save time and money as you reach many more qualified prospects than you would using other marketing and sales methods. Another benefit to telemarketing is that it can be done from anywhere. The person you're calling doesn't know if the call is originating from a Park Avenue office in New York City, someone's home office in Topeka, Kansas, or a massive call center located in downtown Chicago.

To begin making successful calls and "dialing for dollars," a telesales professional needs little more than a telephone. (The fancy office is totally optional.) In addition, when a company focuses on telemarketing as a primary sales tool, fewer people are needed to make more sales. In today's cutthroat and competitive business environment, anything that can be done to reduce costs will impact a company's profitability.

Perhaps the biggest drawback to telemarketing is the lack of face-to-face communication with the prospect. There is no eye contact, no handshake, and no product demonstration (if applicable). You can't show your product or provide a hands-on demonstration, nor can you fix something that's physically broken. Instead, you must rely solely on your verbal communication skills to convey information about the product, set the mood, and develop a bond between you and the prospect. (This is explained in greater detail within Chapter 5 and Chapter 6.)

So, based on the abundance of positive reasons to incorporate telemarketing and telesales into the marketing and sales strategy of your business, should you abandon other proven methods for successfully generating revenues? Absolutely not! What telemarketing can do is allow you to enhance your sales, above and beyond the level they're already at, plus help you streamline your existing sales efforts. Thus, telemarketing should become one component of your overall marketing and sales efforts. Keep in mind, however, that the telephone can be used as a valuable tool for accomplishing a lot more than outbound cold calling.

Cold calling is often considered a primary strategy when telemarketing. In other words, you take a list of prospects who are not currently your customers and who are not expecting your call, and you start calling them, one at a time, and offering your sales pitch over the phone.

For an experienced telemarketer, cold calling is the improper term to associate with this activity. Instead, people skilled in telesales often prefer the term "warm calling," because, before they ever pick up the telephone, they make every effort to prequalify the people or companies they're about to call. Thus, when the telemarketer actually gets the decision-maker on the phone, he or she already knows the prospect has an established need and/or want for the product/service that's being sold. From the telemarketer's perspective, the prospect is already "warm." It's now his or her job to communicate the pertinent information to the prospects and get them to agree that the product/

service is needed, is wanted, would solve a problem, or would somehow fill a void.

As the telemarketer, you should always be excited to be making each call, because you're potentially doing the prospect a favor and/or solving a problem he or she has. You have a product/service that you know will somehow benefit each person you're calling. Every call you make could have a positive impact on the prospect because you're filling a need or want you know already exists. Sure, as the telemarketer you're benefiting yourself and your employer by making a sale, but the product/service you're potentially offering will also benefit the customer. Simply by doing your job, you're creating a win-win scenario. This is the mindset you'll want to adopt.

As the telemarketer, if, in your heart you truly know what you're offering will benefit the prospect, but for whatever reason the prospect doesn't see things your way, perhaps you need to rework your sales pitch or take a different approach. Ask yourself why the person you're trying to sell to isn't understanding the benefits your product/service offers. Is there information you're not properly communicating? Is there something about the prospect's needs you don't understand?

What You Can and Can't Accomplish Using a Telephone

In the remaining chapters of this book, you'll learn what can be accomplished by a skilled telesales professional. At the same time, you'll discover how to develop those skills for yourself. No matter what industry or type of business you're in, the telephone can be used as a tool for:

- ◆ Finding, qualifying, and selling to new customers.
- ◆ Offering top-notch customer service.
- ◆ Generating repeat business from existing customers.

- Identifying problems customers have and fixing them.

- Dealing with customer complaints, then transforming them into happy customers with up-sell potential.

- Fostering relationships and building trust between you and your prospects and customers.

- Setting up appointments to sell a product/service that needs to be demonstrated or used in person (when the product/service can not be sold directly over the telephone).

- Handling technical support calls so customers can better utilize your product/service.

- Participating in conference calls to communicate with several members of an organization, even if they're located in different offices in different cities. Using the telephone, people from around the country or around the world can be gathered together to share thoughts, ideas, and information in real time.

- Accepting verbal orders and taking credit card information as payment. The telephone cannot be used to sign contracts and/or directly accept cash payments. (Some companies can accept checks over the telephone. Contact your bank or financial institution for details about accepting checks by phone.)

In the next chapter, you'll learn about job opportunities for telemarketers, telesales professionals, and customer service representatives. Chapters 4 through 10 will then help you develop your own skills for becoming a successful telemarketer.

Chapter 3

MAKING MONEY
AS A TELEMARKETER

D o you enjoy talking on the phone? Do you consider yourself to be an outgoing person who enjoys meeting new people? Are you generally upbeat? If you answered "yes" to these questions, you already possess some of the most important skills needed to be an effective telesales professional. This chapter explores some of the career opportunities available to inbound and outbound telemarketers. As you'll see, this is one of the few types of jobs where you do not need a graduate or even a four-year college degree to make a very lucrative living.

Just about every company in every industry could benefit from hiring highly skilled telemarketing professionals, whether it's to respond to incoming calls, provide telephone-based customer/technical support, or make outgoing cold calls to generate sales. In addition to working for specific companies, there are also job opportunities available at independent call centers (companies that handle thousands of incoming or outgoing calls per day on behalf of their clients).

Types of Telemarketing/Telesales Jobs

When you think of telesales, you probably think of someone who makes outgoing cold calls in order to generate sales. This is called outbound telemarketing. Anyone in sales should utilize the telephone in some aspects of his or her job in order to save time and money. Ideally, any salesperson could be far more productive if he or she is able to transform some outside sales calls into inside sales using the phone as his or her primary sales tool.

Virtually every type of business can benefit from telemarketing. This opens up a wide range of opportunities for telesales professionals. At one end of the spectrum, there are countless entry-level positions that typically involve selling lower-priced products/services using inbound or outbound telemarketing strategies. For example, this might include selling newspaper subscriptions or long-distance telephone service to consumers. These types of jobs typically pay by the hour and offer only a certain amount of career advancement potential. Higher-level telemarketing and telesales jobs might deal with bigger ticket items, such as advertising, and may offer the telesales professional commissions on their sales. For experienced telemarketers, these jobs can lead to much higher earning potential.

One great thing about this type of career is the advancement opportunity. For example, you could start off selling low-priced ads for a community newspaper and earn an hourly wage. This type of job can help you acquire and hone your core sales skills. Over time, using the same core skills, you could eventually work your way up to selling national magazine advertising or network television advertising, where your earning potential could be far greater because the value of the sales is potentially higher.

There are many types of telephone-based career opportunities for telesales professionals. Some of these jobs include:

Working for a Call Center

This generally involves working in a room with dozens, or perhaps hundreds, of other people either answering calls or making outbound sales calls on behalf of clients. A call center can be found within a large company (in-house) or it could be a separate company that manages calls for a variety of clients. When customers respond to infomercials or choose to place an order from a catalog, for example, they typically call a toll-free 800 number, which gets forwarded to a call center to be answered and processed.

Using the latest technology, companies are now creating virtual call centers. In essence, dozens or even hundreds of people work from their homes. Calls to a company (responding to an 800 number, for example) get forwarded to the telesales professionals at remote locations. A virtual call center links the telesales professionals who are working from different locations together with their employer using computers and the Internet.

Jobs in call centers are typically classified as "Call Center Representative Inbound" or "Call Center Representative Outbound." There are several levels of these positions, starting with entry-level (minimum wage) jobs that typically require little more than a high school education and the ability to read and speak. According to Salary.com (*www.Salary.com*), as of October 2002, the median base salary for this type of position was $23,179, with about half of the job-holders earning between $20,664 and $26,109. The majority of these jobs are compensated by salary alone (as opposed to a salary with bonuses and/or commissions).

A Call Center Representative Level II (Outbound) position, according to Salary.com, involves initiating calls to potential clients using a prepared selling script. This type of position promotes and sells products and services. To land this type of job, an associate's degree or equivalent, along with between two and four years of experience in the field, may be required. Someone applying for this type of job is expected to already be familiar with standard concepts, practices, and procedures within their particular field. A call center representative works under supervision, reporting to a supervisor or manager. The median salary for this type of position is $41,615 (as of October 2002); half of the people holding this type of job earn between $35,440 and $49,581, according to Salary.com.

A Level III or Level IV Outbound Call Center Representative position within a call center is also responsible for initiating calls to potential clients using a prepared selling script in order to sell products/services. This type of job often requires an associate's degree (or its equivalent) with between four and eight years of experience in the field. Someone in this position will report to a supervisor or manager but may also lead and direct the work of others. Salary.com reports: "A wide degree of creativity and latitude is expected." This type of job is often compensation with a salary, plus bonuses and/or commissions. The median salary for this type of job (as of October 2002) was $68,234.

An Outbound Call Center Supervisor is in charge of overseeing employees who place telephone calls to potential customers. Supervisors are responsible for the daily activity of a call center. Landing this type of job typically requires a bachelor's degree as well as several years of experience and the ability to manage others. A supervisor may be considered lower-middle management within an organization. A Call Center Supervisor can earn anywhere from $24,477 to $87,874, depending on the organization and level of responsibility given to him or her.

Inbound Telemarketing

This is a low-pressure job because it does not involve selling. Typically, this type of job involves answering incoming calls;

providing information, customer support, and/or order taking; setting up appointments; or processing requests for more information. The job title often associated with this type of work is Customer Service Representative. Job responsibilities often include processing orders, preparing correspondence, and fulfilling customer needs to ensure customer satisfaction.

Job requirements for this type of position usually include a high school diploma (or equivalent). Some companies may look for some related experience. This type of job typically involves following instructions and pre-established guidelines. Customer Service Representatives often work under direct supervision. According to Salary.com, they earn anywhere from $24,270 to $41,943 (as of October 2002), depending on the industry and their experience.

Outbound Telemarketing

Outbound telemarketing involves calling prospects and selling products/services over the telephone, making collection calls, or setting up appointments for a salesperson to make an in-person sales call. This type of job has a wide salary range, because people are often compensated in a variety of ways (through salary, commission, and/or bonuses). Much of this book focuses on the work of an outbound telesales professional.

Because there are so many job opportunities in telesales, to be successful in this type of job, it's important to first identify an industry and/or company that interests you. This allows you to choose products or services that you truly believe in and feel passionate about. You also need to decide what you want your job responsibilities to be. Are you comfortable making outgoing sales calls, or would you prefer to answer incoming calls (handling customer service-type calls, for example) and not have to do any selling?

Financial Compensation

How people are paid in the telesales field varies dramatically, depending on the industry you're working in, the position you're filling, your job responsibilities, your previous work experience, and your geographic area.

The most common form of compensation is a straight salary. Employees are paid a predetermined flat fee per hour or a weekly salary for a specific number of hours. Benefits may or may not be offered, depending on the employer. Most entry-level telesales jobs involve an hourly, non-commission-based compensation plan.

Some employers award bonuses as a form of compensation to telesales professionals. A bonus can be a flat rate or a percentage of a sale. For example, a bonus may be awarded for reaching a predefined sales goal. A bonus could also be awarded on a per-sale basis. For example, as an outbound telemarketer, you would earn $10 per hour, plus a $1 bonus for each sale you close or each appointment you make.

Higher-level telesales positions often receive commissions as part of their overall compensation package. A commission involves getting paid a predefined percentage of the total sale made. The rate of commission you earn will vary greatly, depending on the industry, company, and product/service you're selling. Some salespeople are also compensated through residuals. This means that once you land a new customer, you continue to receive a commission on all repeat sales for the life of that customer. This can be extremely lucrative for salespeople.

Telemarketers paid entirely or partially by commissions control their own earning potential. The harder they work and the more sales they generate, the higher their income. It's common for (non-entry-level) telesales professionals to be compensated using a combination of salary, bonuses, and commissions. The more experience you have, the more negotiating power you'll have when you seek a telesales job with a new employer.

Yet another form of compensation involves being paid a "draw" as opposed to a straight salary. Unlike a salary, a draw needs to be paid back to the employer, based on commissions earned from future sales. Thus, if you get paid a draw of $100 per week, for example, and for each sale you make you earn $10, you'd need to make 10 sales per week to cover your draw. Any sales you make above the initial 10 sales is money earned by you. If you make 12 sales, you'd earn $120 that week.

Draws can be either refundable or nonrefundable. They're an advance paid by the employer for future sales. A nonrefundable draw means you pay back the draw through sales made over time, but if you resign or are terminated from your job, no money is owed to the employer.

A refundable draw means you owe the employer the money even if you don't cover your draw by making sales. For example, in the beginning of the week, if you're paid a $100 draw and you earn $10 per sale, but that week you make seven sales (earn $70), you'd have to pay back $30 of your draw to the employer. When your draw needs to be paid back is determined in advance by you and the employer. Typically, this will be done on a monthly, quarterly, or semiannual basis. The purpose of a draw is to allow the employee to maintain a regular income he or she can count on, even during slow weeks when fewer sales are made. Some employers will put a cap on the draw they're willing to advance to insure a salesperson doesn't get too far in debt.

For a telesales professional with experience, the ideal compensation plan involves earning a salary, plus commissions and bonuses. For someone who is extremely confident in his or her selling abilities, however, a pure commission-based telesales position can become lucrative, because employers will typically pay a much higher commission for this type of position (mainly because it involves little or no risk for the employer, but a lot of potential risk for the employee).

Before taking on a purely commission-based telephone sales job, make sure you will be able to generate the necessary sales to earn a reasonable income. Keep in mind that, until you establish a client base, it could take several weeks or even months to begin closing larger sales. Thus, there could be a period of time, at least initially, where no income is earned, even though you're working full-time.

Even if you're a highly skilled salesperson, it's often a good strategy to start a new telesales job with a compensation package that involves at least a small salary. With the employer's approval, you could always switch to a pure commission compensation plan later, once you're acclimated at the new company and begin to generate ample sales.

It's important to carefully think through the compensation plan being offered to you before accepting any type of new job. You need to insure that, at the very least, you'll be able to cover your living expenses right from the start, plus determine if the job will ultimately offer the earning potential you need to achieve your short-term and long-term financial goals.

If you accept a telesales job that simply pays $10 per hour, with no bonuses or commissions, there is a predefined maximum income you can earn per day, week, or month in that position. Likewise, if you earn a salary, plus bonuses and/or commissions, you need to calculate your minimum and maximum earning potential. It's always a good idea to speak candidly with other people in your position (working for the same company) to get a realistic idea of the earning potential that's possible.

The cost-of-living calculator, available from the Salary.com Website, is a useful tool for helping to plan your budget, determine your earning potential, and compare what you're being offered in terms of a financial compensation package to what others in your industry and in your geographic area are already being paid. Point your Web browser to *swz.salary.com/ CostOfLivingWizard/layoutscripts/coll_start.asp.*

Hours You Can Expect To Work

Your work schedule will depend on the type of telesales job you land. Jobs in this field are available on a part-time and full-time basis. Depending on the company, you might also be able to choose the shift you work, so daytime, evening, night, and weekend shifts could be available, giving you plenty of flexibility. A lot will also depend on the employer's needs.

If, for example, you're based on the East Coast but you'll be selling to people on the West Coast, you can't begin making calls until 11 a.m. or noon your time, so you may be expected to work until 8 p.m. (EST). Because most telemarketing positions are incentive-based, the more you sell, the more you'll earn. Thus, the number of hours per day, week, or month you work will directly impact your earning potential. Likewise, what you do while you're on the job will also impact your own bottom line. Assuming you're job involves outbound telesales, if you're not on the phone and making calls, you are not earning money.

In many types of outbound telesales jobs, you can control your income, especially if there's a commission or bonus incentive as part of your compensation. In essence, even though you're working for another company, when you're able to earn commissions and/or bonuses, you become your own boss, because you can determine your income based on how hard you work.

Skill Requirements

The skills needed to land a telesales/telemarketing job vary greatly. To land an entry-level job, however, there are minimal prerequisites. The best way to find jobs you're qualified for is to search "help wanted" ads for telemarketing, customer service, and telesales positions to determine exactly what companies are looking for. To review many ads at once, visit a career-related Website, such as The Monster Board (*www.monster.com*), and do a job search. Read the ads carefully. Determine what the employers are looking for and compare your skills, personality, education, and experience to each ad in order to decide which jobs to apply for.

The following are just a few sample ads for telemarketing, customer service, and telesales jobs. Highlighted in bold type are some of the key skills and/or prerequisites each employer is looking for. These are actual ads. The company names and contact information have been changed or deleted. As you'll see, some ads are more descriptive than others.

◆ ◆ ◆

Sample Ad: Telemarketing Position

Telemarketing Positions Available

Fast growing New York City Business-to-Business call center is seeking highly motivated sales people with business experience. We are looking for individuals interested in maximizing their earnings through concentrated, uninterrupted, and focused calling.

Our business is to represent and assist our clients in their sales and marketing campaigns by setting up appointments with prospective customers.

NO SELLING REQUIRED! Just be proficient enough to develop a cold call into a verified qualified lead or appointment by directing the prospect through a series of questions and answers.

We're looking for candidates with a **dynamic personality, strong phone presence, solid cold calling skills** and who are **creative in conversation.** You must have **prior experience in telemarketing or**

phone prospecting. Business experience, internet/ IT background a plus. **You must be comfortable cold calling from our verified lists, creative with scripts, getting information on who the decision-maker is and working with gatekeepers.**

We are offering above average earnings for this profession including salary, commissions, and bonuses. FULL- AND PART-TIME positions available in a 9–5 workweek. We also provide flexible hours for your needs in an informal professional atmosphere.

◆ ◆ ◆

Sample Ad: Telemarketing Position

Immediate opening!

Two positions for healthcare related telemarketing/ data-entry person available:

1. One F/T with benefits: Monday 11 a.m.–7:30 p.m.; Tuesday–Thursday and alternate Saturday/Sunday 12 noon–8:30 p.m.: 40 hours.

2. One P/T: Monday 11 a.m.–3 p.m.; Wednesday–Saturday 4 p.m.–8 p.m.: 20 hours.

If you are a **bright; energetic; independent and outgoing individual** who is interested in "spreading the word" about a new Medicare program now being offered in a growing number of New York Nursing Homes; send us your resume!

Qualified candidates are:

1. **Self-starters.**
2. **Articulate.**

3. **Good listeners.**
4. **Well-organized.**
5. **Computer-savvy: i.e. Microsoft Office (Word, Excel, PowerPoint, Access).**
6. **Outgoing/friendly.**
7. **Highly focused.**
8. **Always professional.**

Experience in healthcare, sales, and/or the needs of frail elders is preferred, but not required.

Salary: F/T: $25,000.00 plus full benefits

P/T: prorated ($12,500.00)

◆ ◆ ◆

Sample Ad: Telesales Position

ABC Company, which offers Web hosting solutions, is seeking professional telesales candidates to join its growing New York City sales team. If you have **prior sales/telesales experience, knowledge of the Internet and a college degree,** you'll find an exciting and rewarding career at ABC Company where your income is equal to your abilities and self-motivation.

ABC Company offers:

◆ A competitive base salary.
◆ An aggressive commissions plan.
◆ Qualified leads.
◆ An entrepreneurial and career-stimulating environment.
◆ Paid training.
◆ Convenient midtown location.

So, if you're interested in helping small businesses and entrepreneurs create their own Websites while jump-starting your own career and income, contact us today.

◆◆◆

Sample Ad: Telesales Position

Outbound Telesales to $40k+

Job Location: Torrance, CA

Job Description: Telesales professionals! Exciting national company is looking for talented closers for this computer sales operation. **The ideal candidate will have 3–5 years of outbound telesales experience.** Generous base plus commission! Send your resume for immediate consideration!

◆◆◆

Sample Ad: Telesales Position

Salary: $25,000.00 to $40,000.00 per year

Position Type: Full Time, Employee

Exciting, growing national organization in Westwood, California seeks a professional to fill our Telemarketing Sales position.

Our sales department continues to exceed expectations with tremendous growth. To support this ongoing growth, we currently have an opportunity available for the right individual.

Requirements/Skills: Essential Duties, Tasks, and Responsibilities:

+ **Achieve assigned key account sales quotas.**

- Originate and develop significant high-level business with portfolio of accounts from established relationships and selected prospects.
- Ensure proper qualification of sales leads/opportunities and provide high quality opportunity management during all phases of the sales cycle.
- Identify customer requirements that may necessitate customized and complex solutions using a wide variety of services and products.
- Provide professional and comprehensive account management of customer accounts.
- Effectively manage customer expectations regarding service features, delivery, and implementation.

Qualifications:

- Superior telephone presentation skills.
- Ability to work with executive level prospects and customers.
- Strong leadership skills and strategic planning.
- Excellent interpersonal and motivating communication skills.
- Self-motivated, energetic, enthusiastic, commitment with a sense of urgency.
- Proven track record in outbound telesales.
- Computer proficiency in Microsoft Office.
- Knowledge of ACT helpful.
- Minimum 5 years experience.

We are in our 5th year with a tremendously success-ful business record and history. We offer our 150-plus staff a competitive salary package including medical, dental, life and long-term disability insur-ance, 401(k) plan, profit sharing plan, bonus op-portunity, 12 paid holidays, and paid time off.

Chapter 4

THE RIGHT SALES MESSAGE IS CRITICAL

The ability to identify your best prospects, deliver your message effectively, and manage your time will directly correlate with the number of sales you make. The more people you call, the more sales you will make. The more you prequalify the people you call, the higher your call-to-sale ratio will be.

By now, you should understand what telemarketing actually is, understand how your company can benefit from the power of telemarketing as a sales tool, and be able to determine the various ways you can incorporate telemarketing into your company's overall sales and marketing efforts.

Knowing this information is the first step to telemarketing success, but there's a lot more you need to accomplish before ever picking up the telephone! We're about to explore the absolute importance of developing the right sales message for the specific prospects to whom you'll soon be telemarketing. You're more apt to experience success if you predefine an effective message and then determine the best approach to take with your prospects.

In this chapter, you'll discover:

- How to define your company's telemarketing sales message.
- How to create a message suitable to be communicated over the telephone.
- How to define your company's overall telemarketing objectives.
- Tips for determining your target audience.
- Proven strategies for matching your sales message to your prospect's needs and wants.
- Hints for getting the customer's attention and keeping it.
- How to predetermine the objections you're bound to encounter.

As you're about to discover, developing the perfect sales message for the product(s)/service(s) your company offers is critical. Even with the right message, however, you still must perfect your presentation and truly understand not just your products/services, but your prospect's wants and needs as well.

Unfortunately, there are no shortcuts when it comes to planning and executing an effective telemarketing campaign. The right approach could easily allow you to:

- Obtain new customers and more repeat customers.
- Drastically improve sales.
- Improve your company's customer relations.
- Enhance your company's reputation and image.
- Increase your company's profits.

If, however, you make mistakes, take the wrong approach, don't understand your objectives, or attempt to take shortcuts, you could easily encounter one hang-up after another when you start making calls, alienate your potential customers, damage your company's reputation, and wind up wasting a lot of time, money, and manpower.

What's Your Company's Sales Message?

From a telemarketer's standpoint, this is a trick question. If you use the same exact sales pitch for every prospect you call, you'll fail as a telemarketer. Although you want to quickly and easily convey all of the benefits of utilizing the product or service you're selling, and at the same time gain the trust of the person you're on the phone with, for example, you also must totally customize your sales pitch to the person you're talking to.

What are the prospect's needs and desires? How can what you're offering help him or her? What are his or her goals and concerns? Forget, for a moment, what you want as a result of the call (a sale), and consider what you can offer to benefit each individual prospect. The cookie-cutter sales approach, where you simply repeat the same script over and over, with no modification, probably isn't going to achieve the results you're looking for.

As you prepare the general sales message you want to convey through your telemarketing efforts, make sure you understand one thing: Your prospect is looking for economic benefit! Whether you're telemarketing to an individual or to a company, you must understand that the person on the other end of the phone is always looking to:

- ✦ Save money.
- ✦ Increase profits (earn more money).
- ✦ Lower costs.
- ✦ Address some other concern or issue.

If you accept this as a universal fact, you can begin to develop a sales message so that it addresses the primary goals of your prospects. Before you begin to discuss what your company can offer to the prospects you're calling, or even make intelligent recommendations, you must understand at least the basics of who your potential client is and what business he or she is in (if you're telemarketing to other companies).

When telemarketing to companies, before picking up the phone, you should already know the answers to the following questions:

- ◆ What business is your prospect in?
- ◆ Who are your prospect's competitors?
- ◆ How does your prospect make money?
- ◆ What are the challenges your prospect faces?
- ◆ What is your prospect concerned about day after day?

If you're telemarketing to individuals, you'll want to know similar information about your prospects, including answers to these questions:

- ◆ What problems or concerns can you help the prospect address and solve?
- ◆ How can your product(s)/service(s) help your prospect earn more money, save money, save time, reduce stress, or alleviate a concern?

Your company's sales message must address these issues and focus on promoting the benefits of your product(s)/service(s) to your prospects. In order to do this successfully, it's important that you, as the telemarketer, know what you're selling inside and out. You must also know your own competition and be able to communicate why what you're offering is a better alternative.

As the telemarketer, it's important to truly believe in what you're selling. Only then will you sound genuine, confident, and believable as you talk to prospects. If you don't believe what you're saying, this will become very obvious on the phone and you'll quickly lose credibility. When you think of a "salesperson" the image that probably comes to mind is someone who talks fast and is insincere and perhaps even dishonest. This is the stereotypical image you absolutely do not want to convey.

Now that you have a basic understanding of what your company's sales message needs to incorporate, start to develop some ideas for your overall sales presentation. Once you've created what you think is the perfect telephone sales message, the next obstacle will be to get prospects to stay on the phone long enough for you to present it.

Remember that nobody likes to be sold something. However, everyone likes to make an intelligent buy. Think about how you personally feel after you've gotten a great bargain at the store. Most people are so excited they actually brag about their purchase to friends and relatives, thus creating word-of-mouth referrals and additional business for the company.

As you develop a sales presentation for your company, it's important for your prospect to develop a perceived value for what you're offering. If he or she doesn't see the value, you have not done a good sales job, and you'll either lose the prospect or wind up having to put forth an incredible effort to overcome all of his or her objections and concerns. As the telemarketer, it's always your job to create perceived value for what you're selling.

Always be specific! When you are on the telephone, your prospect cannot see you, your sales literature, or your product(s)/service(s). Thus, as you talk on the phone and describe what you offer, it's important that your sales message utilize highly descriptive language that will make what you're selling more interesting, more alive, and more appealing. Using descriptive language is not the same, however, as using complex language or too much technical jargon that will ultimately confuse, frustrate, or bore the person you're speaking with.

Part of your preparation should include creating an informal agenda for every call. On paper (or using a computer), list your primary selling points, important notes, and/or the actual script of what you plan to say.

It will become important for your prospects to know that they are ultimately buying into a relationship with you first, and then the product(s)/service(s) you're actually selling. Thus, it's your responsibility to begin building strong relationships with your prospects right from the start.

Ultimately, you'll discover that the relationship between the customer and the sales representative is crucial for obtaining sales and later repeat sales. Buyers stick with salespeople who give them the best service and the most personalized attention and who address their individual needs. Top salespeople and telemarketers deliver more than they promise; provide outstanding service before, during, and after the sales; and offer value-added services to their customers.

Communicating Over the Telephone

Telemarketing can be as powerful as an in-person sales presentation, however, when you're utilizing the telephone as a sales tool, you have no visuals at your disposal. The prospect cannot see or touch whatever you're attempting to sell. Thus, what you say, how you say it, and the emotion and intensity conveyed with your voice become all the more important.

To be an effective telemarketer, you need to be able to communicate well verbally but also master the art of listening. The ideal sales call should involve the following phases:

+ Make opening statements.
+ Ask questions.
+ Develop an understanding of your prospect:
  Where is he or she now? What is his or her
  vision for the future?

- Listen to what the prospect has to say, and observe his or her behavior.
- Take notes, but always remain attentive. You'll want to remember exactly what the prospect had to say during each call.
- Qualify the prospect's needs and wants.
- Repeat some of what the prospect tells you to demonstrate your understanding.
- Eliminate the prospect's objections and concerns.
- Offer your solutions to the prospect's needs and problems.
- Create a win/win situation.
- Offer value added services as the salesperson.
- Close the sale.

Virtually anything can be sold or marketed using the telephone. For those few situations where the prospect absolutely must see or touch a product firsthand, for example, you can use telemarketing to qualify prospects, generate interest, and set up in-person sales meetings. The very best telemarketers develop the skills needed to close sales without ever meeting in-person with the client, yet they offer the personalized attention that allows for a strong, long-term business relationship to develop.

Just as with in-person selling, first impressions are important. Instead of making judgments based on how you look, however, when you're telemarketing the person you're speaking with will develop his or her impression of you based upon what you say and how you sound. Use your voice to its fullest advantage. The tone of your voice, your pronunciation, the volume at which you speak, and how you place emphasis on certain words and phrases will help you underline important points and communicate in an authoritative, yet emphatic way. (This will be explained in greater detailed in Chapter 6.)

Defining Your Objective(s)

Without thinking for more than a second or two, you should be able to state that the primary objective of your telemarketing efforts is to increase sales and ultimately boost profits. What are some of your other objectives as a telemarketer? As you answer this question, remember to think beyond your own needs and to once again consider the needs of your prospects.

Before you begin your telemarketing efforts, it's important to understand exactly what you're trying to accomplish and how you plan to achieve those objectives. Who are you going to be calling? What are you going to say? How are you going to say it? What do you want the immediate outcome of each phone call to be? What do you want the long-term benefits of your telemarketing efforts to be?

Determining Your Target Audience

You can start your telemarketing efforts right now by opening a telephone book (the White Pages if you're marketing to individuals, or the Yellow Pages if you're telemarketing to businesses) and start making calls. Starting with the first entry in the telephone book and working your way from A to Z is one approach, but is this the best approach to take? No!

The people you call should be prequalified as being within your target audience. If you truly understand your product(s)/service(s), you should easily be able to determine exactly what type of individual or company will get the most benefit out of what you have to offer. These are the people most apt to buy what you're selling. This is your target audience.

Next, develop your telemarketing prospect list based on the criteria you define. This will allow you to somewhat prequalify your prospects and achieve far greater results with less effort on your part. For example:

- ◆ If you're targeting males, between the ages of 18 and 49, with an income level of $35,000 or higher, you don't want to waste valuable time and resources calling women who live alone, older males, or low-income households.

- ◆ If you're trying to sell home mortgage refinancing services to people, you don't want to call people who don't already own a home or who don't have an existing mortgage.

- ◆ If you're selling chimney-sweeping services to homeowners, it's important to acquire a list of prospects who have fireplaces or chimneys that need to be cleaned. Don't bother to call people living in apartments with no fireplaces or chimneys.

Later (in Chapter 13) you'll learn about how to purchase or rent reliable prospect lists. Even once you've developed your prequalified list, as you start to make calls you'll need to use your charm and information gathering skills to insure you're actually speaking with the right person: the decision-maker. You'll discover it's easy to waste a lot of time and energy telemarketing to people who are not qualified to make the final "buying" decision.

During the early stages of a telemarketing call, you can determine if you're speaking to the right person—the decision-maker—by asking very simple questions, such as, "Mr. (insert name of prospect), if you like what you hear, who else will we need to share this information with in order to go forward?"

In order to make sales, you need to first identify and then sell to the decision-maker. Who this person is, especially if you're telemarketing to companies, isn't always obvious. You might be required to ask multiple questions in order to identify all of the individuals you'll ultimately need to convince before a sale can be made.

To reach all of the right people, you may need to ask for help from the people you speak with, collect names and titles, and ask several questions. If you discover that four or five people are all part of the decision-making process, your goal should be to establish a conference call with all of these people. This will save time and confusion and eliminate the need to sell by phone to each person individually.

Matching Your Message to Your Prospect's Wants and Needs

Depending on the product or service you're selling, your target audience may be the mass market (virtually everyone from anywhere). It's more likely, however, to be a specific portion of the population, a narrowly defined niche market, or a specific type of company.

In terms of telemarketing to individuals, your target audience may be defined in any number of ways, such as by their sex, age, income, geographic area, education level, occupation, family make-up, interests/hobbies, ethnic background, religion, political beliefs, favorite activities, and so forth. The more information you have about who your target customers are, the easier it will ultimately be to reach them with your marketing message and better cater your product(s) or service(s) to them.

Telemarketing can be extremely successful for niche or specialized marketing activities. This means reaching a very specific audience with your company's marketing, advertising, and public relations message. Once you understand who your audience is and what exact information you need or want to convey to this audience, you'll be able to pinpoint very specific, cost-effective ways of reaching your target customers using the telephone.

The following questions will help you better understand your target audience if you'll be telemarketing to individuals as opposed to companies. Although your company and its product(s)/service(s) may appeal to many different types of people or companies, try to focus on who your primary target customer will be as you answer the following questions. You can later go back and answer the same questions again to define a secondary customer base.

- Does your product/service appeal to primarily males or females?
- What is the age range of your target customer?
- Where does your target customer live? In a major city, the suburbs, in what state(s) or regions? Does he or she live in a home, apartment, condo, retirement home, trailer park?
- What is your target customer's family situation (unmarried, married, married with children, married with teenagers, divorced)?
- How much education does your target customer have (high school graduate, college graduate, advanced degree, specific license/accreditation)?
- What type of job or career does your average customer have (homemaker, minimum-wage job, middle management, executive-level, part-time worker)?
- What is the average income of your target customer?
- What is your target customer's race and/or religion (if applicable)?
- Where does your target customer typically shop? How often? How much does he or she spend?
- What does your target customer do for fun? What hobbies does he or she have?
- How does your target customer spend his or her free time?

- How much time does your target customer spend at home, in his or her car, at work?
- Does your target customer currently use product(s) or service(s) offered by your competitors? If so, how can you get him or her to switch?
- Is your product/service something that your target audience needs, wants, or needs and wants?

Based on how you answered these questions, spend time developing a one- or two-sentence synopsis of who your target customer is and then carefully define what exact marketing message(s) you want to reach these people with in order to tell them about your company's product(s)/service(s) and create a need and demand for what your company has to offer. If your telemarketing efforts are ultimately going to be successful, the primary message you attempt to convey to your target must be consistent and directly relevant to the customer's needs and wants.

Whether you'll be telemarketing to individuals or businesses, describe your target audience in between one and three sentences here:

Getting the Customer's Attention and Keeping It

From the moment you make contact with a prospect on the telephone, you know what your objective is (and he or she knows what your objective is: to sell something to him or her).

To increase you chances of capturing the attention of the prospect, quickly and succinctly answer the prospect's question, "What's in it for me?"

When a prospect answers the phone, you, as the telemarketer, are interrupting whatever he or she was doing. If he was in the middle of something important, he might even be a bit annoyed at the intrusion. Right at the start, ask the prospect if she has a minute to speak. If she is too busy to talk, ask when a better time would be. Make a specific phone appointment to call back. Then, when you do call back, you'll know you have a predefined appointment, the person is expecting the call and you don't have to worry about bothering him or her.

In the first 10, 20, or 30 seconds of the conversation, your objective is not to talk fast enough to communicate your entire sales message. All you need to do initially is relax, speak calmly and clearly, and get the prospect's attention. Once you've gotten the person's attention (which you need to do right away), you'll then have the time you need to properly make your presentation. Without being rude, you'll need to be creative and develop a way to demand the prospect's attention right away. Only by getting the person on the other end of the phone to keep listening will you be able to make your entire presentation.

During the first few seconds of the call, you'll want to achieve the following:

- Identify yourself and your organization in a friendly and upbeat manner.
- State why you are calling and offer a benefit.
- Ask a question or make a statement that will quickly get the prospect involved in the conversation.

**Sample Telemarketing Call
Opening Statement**

"Hello, Mr. Smith. I'm Claudia from The XYZ Corporation. We help companies increase their sales by providing advertising services. I was flipping through the pages of The Boston Globe and noticed your ad in the July 14th edition. How has the response been to this ad?"

In just a few quick sentences, this opening statement introduced the caller, offered a benefit ("We help companies increase their sales") and asked a question ("How has the response been to this ad?")." Remember: It's important to start off by providing a reason for the call, not a hard-core sales pitch.

Before you start making calls, pretend for a few minutes that you are the prospect. Ask yourself if you would be responsive to the opening lines of the sales presentation or script you've created. If you answered "no," keep working until you come up with something that would grab your attention. Think about telemarketing calls you've received. What did the salesperson say that kept you on the phone or that made you want to hang up?

There are many ways a telemarketer can fail to achieve his or her goals. For example, the telemarketer could lack enthusiasm, lack confidence, and/or demonstrate product ambivalence. Be sure you avoid these common pitfalls, and keep in mind that there's a big difference between a telemarketer being professional and persistent, as opposed to pushy.

Even after you make an initial sale, keep the relationship you've developed strong. This could lead to repeat sales, the ability to up-sell, or to obtaining referrals for other prospects. Thus, it's important to stay in contact with your clients. One of the biggest mistakes telemarketers make is to neglect their clients once the initial sale is made. Check in with the client periodically. Send thank-you notes or gifts, send holiday cards, and so on.

Predicting Objections in Advance and Dealing With Them

If you know your product(s)/service(s) intimately and you've done your research about your target audience, you should then be able to determine what each of your prospect's primary objections will be *before* you ever pick up the telephone. By accurately predicting these objections and concerns, you can address them as part of your sales presentation before they're ever brought up by the prospect. A good telemarketer will deal with all objections so the prospect never feels the need to bring them up.

Five of the most common objections you'll encounter as a telemarketer are:

1. "Your rates are too high."
2. "Let me think it over."
3. "I have to check with my partner/wife/ husband."
4. "My budget is already spent."
5. "The economy is terrible, so business is bad. I can't spend any money now."

Here are some common ways of addressing these objections within your sales presentation:

1. "Your rates are too high." Possible solution: "I really must apologize to you. I really haven't done a good enough job explaining why my services

are worth these rates. Let me show you why this program will prove to be cost-effective for you."

2. "Let me think it over." Possible solution: "I understand. You don't want to make a quick decision. Mr. Prospect, tell me: What exactly is it that you need to think about?"

3. "I have to check with my partner/wife/husband." Possible solution: "Why not speak with them right now and get that okay so we can go forward right away?"

4. "My budget is already spent." Possible solution: "If you did have the budget, would you start right away?" [Assuming a "yes" response: "Great. Then let's find the dollars we need."]

5. "The economy is terrible, so business is bad. I can't spend any money now." Possible solution: "Your competitors are going through the same tough times as you are. I have some specific plans that will help increase your sales and make your business stronger. Let's make sure your business is on top as the economy improves."

Take a few moments and write down what you believe the top five objections or concerns will be among your prospects once you begin your telemarketing efforts. Next, for each objection or concern you've listed, come up with at least three ways you can overcome it.

To eliminate objections before they occur, ask questions, identify a need, verify the need exists with the client, and then offer a solution. This process should dramatically cut down or eliminate a lot of the objections.

Top 5 Anticipated Objections

Objection #1: _____

_____

_____

    Solution #1: _____

    _____

    _____

    Solution #2: _____

    _____

    _____

    Solution #3: _____

    _____

    _____

Objection #2: _____

_____

_____

    Solution #1: _____

    _____

    _____

    Solution #2: _____

    _____

    _____

    Solution #3: _____

    _____

    _____

Objection #3: _____

_____

_____

    Solution #1: _____

    _____

    _____

    Solution #2: _____

    _____

    _____

    Solution #3: _____

    _____

    _____

Objection #4: _____

_____

_____

    Solution #1: _____

    _____

    _____

    Solution #2: _____

    _____

    Solution #3: _____

    _____

    _____

Objection #5: _____

_____

_____

    Solution #1: _____

    _____

    _____

    Solution #2: _____

    _____

    _____

    Solution #3: _____

    _____

    _____

If one of your prospects hasn't made the "buy" decision by the time your sales presentation comes to a close, chances are there is some type of concern or objection that's still lingering in his or her mind.

When an objection does arise, isolate it, overcome it, and then try to close the sale. If the answer is "no," determine which objection(s) still remain, isolate each of them, offer solutions to each of them, then try to close the sale again. Keep following this procedure until the prospect's choice is totally clear and he or she chooses to become a valued client.

Remember: When a prospect gives you an objection, he or she feels that he or she has a legitimate concern about what you're offering. Never imply that the prospect is wrong for having a concern, by making a statement such as, "Yes, but...."

Instead, approach his or her concern or objection using the "feel, felt, found" approach. Upon listening to the prospect's objection or concern, make a statement along the lines of, "I understand how you feel. Other have felt that same way, but they have found that...."

In addressing the concern, ask questions. Confront the objection head-on and deal with it. Repeat the objection to the customer (to show you understand it), then ask the prospect *why* this is a major concern.

Next ask, "If I can resolve this issue, are you ready to go forward?" At this point, the response should be "yes." Now, confront the objection and present strategies for alleviating that concern based on the benefits of your product(s)/service(s). Turn the objection into a question, then respond to the objection. If multiple objections come up, choose the easiest ones to address and solve first.

Throughout your sales presentation, keep the prospect agreeing with your statements and keep him or her talking. For example, let's assume you're selling newspaper advertising space. During the course of your conversation, you determine that the only way you'll make a sale is if the prospect's ad appears opposite the Sports section, the cost of the ad doesn't exceed $1,000 per week, and that the copy for the ad can be changed often without incurring additional typesetting or layout costs.

Upon determining this information, make statements such as, "Let me make sure I am clear, Mr. Smith. If we can get you advertising space in the newspaper that is opposite the Sports section, this would be of interest? You want to have the flexibility to change your ad on a frequent basis at no additional cost? Your weekly budget is $1,000 per week?" Thus far, you should have received several "yes" responses in a row. Now ask, "So, assuming we can accomplish this, you'd like to insert your ad in our newspaper for the next year?"

If there's ever information you, as the telemarketer/ salesperson do not know, don't be afraid to tell the prospect that you'll research the answer and call him or her back at a predefined time. Make sure you follow up with them promptly. When you call the prospect back, identify yourself, then tell him or her you have great news. You have obtained the information he or she was looking for. This will build your credibility and trust, plus demonstrate you're doing everything possible to address the prospect's needs and concerns. In addition, the prospect will feel like you've done him or her a favor.

Wrapping it Up and Closing the Sale

Depending on what you're trying to sell and who your prospects are, you'll quickly establish a pattern for each and every one of your calls. From start to finish, every call you make will probably include:

1. Making an opening statement whereby you introduce yourself and your company. (This is who we are. This is what we do.)
2. Offering a benefit.
3. Asking questions.
4. Listening.
5. Getting agreement.
6. Taking notes.
7. Trying to close the sale.
8. Handling objections.
9. Getting agreement.
10. Trying to close the sale again.

Remember: Nothing is more important than understanding your customers, knowing the product(s)/service(s) you're trying to sell, being able to communicate the benefits to your prospects, building up trust, and developing a positive relationship.

From this chapter you learned how to determine what you need to say during each call as you develop your sales presentation. In the next chapter, we'll explore how important your attitude is when it comes to being a successful telemarketer and actually closing sales.

Chapter 5

YOUR ATTITUDE IS EVERYTHING

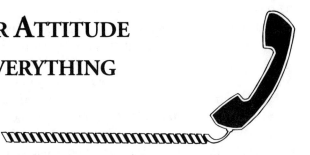

I t's true: Telemarketing, particularly outbound telesales, is all about picking up the phone and making calls to qualified prospects. In addition to developing the right message for your sales pitch, however, how you ultimately present it will have a tremendous impact on your success.

This chapter focuses on the importance of developing and maintaining the right attitude when "dialing for dollars." Even though the people you're calling can't see you, they can hear you, so your attitude will be communicated. From your own perspective, it's also important to maintain the proper attitude when dealing with various types of prospects and clients to insure that you don't become stressed out, annoyed, or frustrated. These negative emotions will impact your morale and ultimately impact the buying decision of your prospects.

Developing the Right Attitude

When you contact a prospect, chances are he or she is busy. At the very least, he or she is in the process of dealing with the trials and tribulations in his or her own life. So, be sure that whatever negative personal or professional issues you're dealing with don't get communicated over the phone. If necessary, spend a few minutes at the start of your workday meditating, working out, or doing whatever is necessary to get into the proper frame of mind for the task ahead.

When telemarketing, focus on the task at hand. Maintain an upbeat, cheerful, and positive attitude that is conducive to selling. After all, if you're making outbound cold calls, the people you're contacting didn't ask for your call, they don't know you, and you interrupted whatever it is they were doing when you called. Likewise, if someone calls your company looking to place an order or obtain information, for example, the last thing he or she wants to do is talk to someone who sounds angry or frustrated or who lacks focus.

Whether you're making or receiving your first call or your hundredth call of the day, your attitude must remain constantly upbeat and enthusiastic, even if you've received a dozen or more rejections in a row. The most subtle changes in your attitude will be subconsciously communicated over the phone, and you want to avoid that. Remember: People can't see you. Assuming you can get the prospect to stay on the phone long enough to listen to your pitch, he or she will easily be able to tell if you're excited about what you're saying or if you're simply reading a script you've been repeating to each prospect you call.

Throughout your day, evaluate your mood and attitude and make adjustments as necessary. If you're in a bad mood, frustrated, or lacking enthusiasm, you're more apt to be rude to prospects, offers harsh responses instead of friendly ones, maintain a mean scowl on your face (as opposed to a smile), grit your teeth, have trouble concentrating, lack follow-through, and possibly have a far more difficult time engaging in productive conversations. As a result, you'll quickly turn off your prospects to whatever you're offering. If you find yourself doing anything that isn't 100-percent conducive to helping you make a sale, you need to take a break and refocus your energies.

As each and every caller hangs up the phone after speaking with you, that person should believe that you're positive, upbeat, friendly, intelligent, and able to properly represent your company and that you posses extensive knowledge about what you're selling. Your prospects need to believe not just that you know what you're taking about, but also that you truly believe what you're saying about the product/service and that you have a genuine interest in helping him or her.

Getting Into the Right Frame of Mind

Let's face it, there will be days when you simply don't want to be happy and cheerful. There will be times when, for personal or professional reasons, you have other things on your mind than selling your product/service. In these situations, before dealing with prospects and/or clients on the telephone, you need to get into the proper frame of mind. This means blocking outside influences, getting in a cheerful and motivated mood, and focusing exclusively on the task at hand.

There are many ways for people to motivate themselves and change their attitude, including:

- Before picking up the phone, envision yourself achieving success and closing sales. Visualize yourself succeeding.

- Determine and then remove the roadblocks that are holding you back from developing and maintaining the attitude you need to achieve success. Competency and confidence are two key elements that allow salespeople to achieve success. If you have both, other obstacles can be overcome.

- Focus on how you felt the last time you made a sale and recapture that feeling as you embark on making new calls.

- Focus on solutions, not on problems. Likewise, concentrate on achieving success as opposed to worrying about failure.

- If you're a manager or supervisor of a telemarketing team, develop a daily or weekly reward system or method of recognition for your top achievers. Give people something to work toward and motivate them with a friendly competition.

- Keep rewarding yourself for the successes you achieve in order to stay motivated and focused.

- Listen to tapes of a motivational speaker or read something that you find motivational.

- Listen to upbeat music. This will help to motivate you.

- Reinforce in your mind that by making sales, you're not just helping yourself and your company; you're also helping your customers, because what you're offering can benefit them or will help them solve a problem.

- Review your personal goals and objectives and focus on why you developed these goals. Make sure the goals you have are attainable. If, for example, you're saving money for a new car, dream vacation, or dream house, picture that objective in your mind. Focus on the positive aspects of what you're trying to achieve for yourself (as well as your company). All by itself, money isn't generally a motivating factor for people. Instead, once you earn the money as a result of making sales, focus your thoughts on what will be purchased with the money. Everyone has their own goals that motivate them. It's important to determine what yours are early on and stay focused on them.

- ◆ Take a few moments to meditate and clear your mind after a particularly difficult or frustrating call.

- ◆ Understand that the effort you make will lead directly to your performance as a telesales professional. The right performance level will result in the rewards you're looking for. Thus, if you know what's required to achieve the desired results, you're more apt to be motivated to put forth the necessary effort. Greater efforts lead to better performance and better performance leads to greater rewards. Obtaining the rewards, in turn, will motivate you to put forth greater effort. It's an endless cycle.

- ◆ Use the buddy system to motivate yourself and your coworkers. Share success stories and be able to vent about the negative aspects of your job or situation in order to work through them and move on. Try to surround yourself with positive people who inspire and support you.

Your Attitude Is Communicated by Your Voice and Body Language

Once you have your sales pitch developed, grab a tape recorder and, as you're rehearsing, try the following experiment. Present your script (during a rehearsal or role-play exercise) with a big smile on your face. Also, use body language as you make your presentation and allow your positive emotions to emanate from you. Next, rehearse your pitch again (also recording it). This time, however, do it with a frown on your face and refrain from using body language. Also, keep your emotions in check.

Now, rewind the tape, close your eyes, and imagine you're the prospect on the other end of the phone. Listen carefully to both of your presentations. Can you hear the distinct difference in your voice and in the attitude you conveyed? As the prospect, which presentation would you be more apt to make a buying decision after hearing?

Because you don't have the luxury of being seen during a sales call, what you communicate over the phone is extremely important. Thus, even if you look foolish because you have an extra large smile on your face during each call, your prospect can't see you, but he or she will hear the joy in your voice—and that's what's important because you want that person to come away feeling good about the conversation.

If your supervisor were to ask each of your prospects to describe you after your call, ideally, the following words should be used:

- Caring.
- Concerned.
- Confident.
- Credible.
- Enthusiastic.
- Friendly.
- Genuine/Sincere.
- Knowledgeable.
- Positive.
- Reliable.

These are not simply words. To achieve success as a telemarketer or telesales professional, the attitude you develop and maintain with your prospects and clients will correlate directly with your level of success. Evaluate your own professional personality and attitude and make sure that the person your prospects perceive you to be is actually along the lines of what you want it to be. Otherwise, you need to make adjustments fast.

As important as it is, however, to convey the right emotions and attitude when you speak, it's equally important to listen carefully to what each prospect or client has to say, especially when he or she is voicing an opinion or concern. In these situations, it's your responsibility to genuinely express concern, understanding, and/or empathy for what's being said. This can be done easily by acknowledging your understanding and repeating or paraphrasing what the prospect just said. Always choose your words carefully so that the message you're communicating is clear and so you can more easily create a sense of agreement between yourself and the prospect.

By demonstrating knowledge about what you're selling as well as an understanding of your prospect's needs and wants, you'll have an easier time conveying the proper attitude. In addition to the attitude you convey to prospects and clients, the attitude that's in your heart as a telemarketer should involve persistence.

Be Persistent, But Don't Be a Pest

You already know you'll save a lot of time and frustration by prequalifying your prospects before making calls. Once you identify a good prospect, the next step is to get yourself on the phone with the right decision-maker. When telemarketing to other businesses, there will be times when you call a particular company and you get to someone who isn't being receptive to what you're saying. Don't give up too quickly and cross them off your prospect list.

This is where persistence and the right attitude will come in handy. If you're dealing with someone in a particular department and he or she isn't receptive to what you're selling, but you know the company you're calling is a viable prospect, you might want to call back a bit later and try to learn what the problem is. When you do this, put the blame on yourself. Say, "I must not be doing a good job explaining what I have to offer, because I truly believe what I'm selling can benefit your company. What information do you need from me to demonstrate that what I have can be beneficial to you and your company?"

If you're dealing with a closed-minded person and you have exhausted your efforts with that person, consider working your way up one rung on the corporate ladder and talk to that person's boss. Start your sales pitch again, but be sure to put the person you initially spoke with in a good light. You might be able to spark the interest of someone higher up within the company. As you do this, you don't want to burn any bridges, so try to keep everyone in the loop.

Even after contacting several people within an organization, you may, for whatever reason, not be able to close a sale, even if you're convinced the prospect is highly qualified. In this situation, keep the prospect on your follow-up list and stay in touch with him or her. Down the road, try sending or faxing information periodically that might spark his or her interest, then call back sometime in the future.

It is a very rare occasion when you will make a sale on the very first call to a prospect. In most cases, it will take several phone calls, during which you'll need to answer many questions and deal with one or more people within the organization before a decision is made. Throughout this process, maintaining the proper attitude and being consistent is critical. If you are persistent with your prospects over a period of time, it helps to demonstrate that you're not going anywhere and that you're reliable. You can foster the prospect's confidence in you by following through on everything you promise. For example, if someone asks you to call him or her back in a week, be sure to make an appointment on your calendar, and then make that follow up call at the appropriate time. Likewise, if you promise to send out literature, it's important to do this in a timely manner. After all, prospects will look at your follow through during this phase of the relationship as a preview of what can be expected in terms of customer service once they decide to become a customer.

Establish Agreement Between You and Your Prospects

Even in situations where the people you're calling disagree with what you're saying during your sales pitch, part of your job as a salesperson involves creating a sense of agreement, first on smaller issues and then on the bigger ones. Each time you develop an understanding and agreement on an issue or topic, you're one step closer to closing a sale.

During your pitch, don't be afraid to ask for agreement. If, for example, you're selling advertising to a business, say something along the lines of, "When you implement our advertising program, it will become a cost-effective part of your marketing mix. If I can show you how your company will increase sales by implementing my program, would you want to go ahead with it?" Of course, as the telemarketer, you already know the answer to this obvious question. If you can, without a doubt, prove your advertising program works and will increase sales for the prospect, you know he or she will participate. The goal, however, is to create a verbal agreement with the prospect/ client. Doing this as part of your pitch will help to keep the conversation flowing, generate greater interest in what you're offering, and help insure that you and your prospect are on the same page.

In order to generate a sense of agreement, as the salesperson, you must also establish trust with your prospects. Communicating the appropriate attitude, plus demonstrating that you (and your company) will be around for a long time in the future to offer top-notch customer service and support, will go a long way toward building that trust.

Keep in mind that part of your job as a telemarketer involves dealing with rejection. In order to close a single sale, you'll most likely receive multiple "no's" along the way. Even when you personally feel rejected or frustrated, it's critical that these emotions don't get communicated to prospects. Likewise, you never want to come across as desperate. The prospects you're calling should each feel as though they're your first call of the day. Your pitch should sound always fresh. One way to achieve this is to develop several versions of your sales pitch. Throughout the day, switch between your pitches in order to add variety and break the monotony for yourself. Remember that every "no" is one step closer to a "yes."

Chapter 6

Speak Up! Using Your Voice as a Sales Tool

As a telemarketer or telesales professional, there are many skills from your professional skill set you will be called upon to utilize on a daily basis in order to close sales. One tool you'll come to rely heavily on is your voice. After all, this is what will be used to communicate over the telephone to prospects, clients, and customers. This chapter focuses on all aspects of using your voice as a sales tool. Even if you're already a good verbal communicator, there is always room for improvement and, as with any new skill, learning to properly use your voice as a powerful sales tool will take practice.

How Your Voice Impacts Your Ability to Succeed

Just about everyone has received calls from telemarketers at their home. As the recipient of a telemarketing call, you have two options: You can hang up immediately or you can listen to the sales pitch. What are the factors involved when you decide to listen to a sales pitch? Two possibilities include:

- ◆ You have an interest in what's being sold.
- ◆ You've been captivated by the way the telemarketer communicates. He or she used his or her voice to create an almost instant bond with you.

As the recipient of a telemarketing call, how many times have you almost instantly hung up the phone, because you realized the telemarketer was simply reading a prewritten script, conveyed no excitement about what he or she was saying, and had trouble properly communicating why he or she was calling or what he or she was selling?

In the business world, first impressions are critical! As a telemarketer, someone can't see what you look like, your hairstyle, how well you're dressed, or how well you carry yourself, so the people you call upon must rely solely on your verbal communication skills—that is, what you say and how you say it. If you don't immediately present yourself as someone who is friendly, intelligent, and offering the receiver of the call something he or she wants or needs, your chances of keeping someone on the line for more than a few seconds are slim at best.

If you were to attend an important business meeting in a corporate environment, what would go though your mind if the person you were meeting with for the first time showed up wearing ripped jeans and a dirty T-shirt as opposed to a nicely tailored and clean business suit? That person might be smart and competent, but chances are that his or her credibility would be instantly lost with you, as a direct result of your first impression of that unprofessional and inappropriately dressed person. The same rule applies for telemarketers who don't properly use their voice, not just to make that all-important first impression, but to constantly captivate the attention of the prospect or customer throughout the length of each and every call.

Learning to Control Your Voice

Actors, radio personalities, politicians, and public speakers from all walks of life spend years enhancing and perfecting their verbal communication skills through practice, rehearsing, and training. As a telemarketer or telesales professional, how you use your voice can become one of your biggest assets. Everyone's voice is as unique as their personality and appearance. If used properly, it will impress people, be remembered, allow you to build positive business relationships over the phone, and help you convey information.

Your ability to master the art of verbal communication encompasses several elements, including:

- **Volume** (how loudly or softly you speak).
- **Vocabulary** (the words you use to communicate).
- **Pronunciation** (your ability to use the English language correctly).
- **Speed of delivery** (how fast or slowly you speak).
- **Conveying emotions** (using your voice to convey confidence, sincerity, intelligence, enthusiasm, joy, friendliness, concern, anger, annoyance, frustration, fright, nervousness, depression, or any other emotion).

These are the key elements that need to be perfected in order to become a skilled speaker. Just as important, however, is your ability to listen to what others have to say. In terms of telemarketing, once you've qualified your prospects and created your pitch, your ability to succeed will depend on how well you're able to communicate. For example, as you present your pitch, you could use the right words (vocabulary), the appropriate volume and pronunciation, but lack the emotion needed to properly engage the person you're speaking with. Likewise, if you speak too fast, the person you're talking to might not be able to keep up; if you speak too slowly, you run the risk of boring the prospect or client. If your voice lacks emotion, it will seem as if you don't care about what you're saying or you don't truly believe it, which will have a negative impact on the prospect or client. If you use the wrong words or clearly don't know the proper meaning of the vocabulary you're using, you could come across as lacking intelligence or say something confusing. Thus, to achieve success as a verbal communicator, all of these speech elements need to work together seamlessly during each and every phone call you make.

When you engage in an in-person conversation, it's normal to use body language and facial expressions to emphasize what you're saying. When engaged in telephone sales, these same gestures and facial expressions are important, because they'll prevent your voice from taking on a monotonous sound. In addition to using gestures, even though they can't be seen, you must add energy to your voice in order to communicate properly. In fact, during a call, feel free to stand up as you make your sales pitch. Using a telephone headset frees up your hands and gives you added mobility, allowing you to better express yourself. Just as actors often spend weeks rehearsing their lines before a performance to make their character more believable, you, too, should rehearse how you present your sales pitch, so that your presentation is natural, engaging, and believable.

Volume

Adding volume to your speech or changing your tone can be used to convey important points and capture someone's attention. You might want to raise the volume of your voice or lower its tone slightly when making an important point in order to add emphasis, for example.

When you're giving your sales pitch, make sure the prospect has no trouble hearing you. If the volume of your voice is too soft, the person you're speaking with might misinterpret that as fear, or nervousness or that you have a meek personality. Likewise, if you speak too loudly, it could be interpreted that you're pushy or domineering. The volume of your voice should be consistent with an everyday conversation, however, the pitch of your voice and the emotions you convey should be more powerful than if you're sitting face-to-face with someone having a conversation.

Vocabulary

Many studies have shown that someone's command of the English language is directly related to how he or she is perceived in the business world and to the level of career advancement he or she is able to achieve. This is because how well you communicate verbally impacts the perception people develop about you. If you speak well, it will automatically be assumed you're well-educated and intelligent. Developing a strong command of the English language doesn't necessarily mean using thousands of obscure and fancy words in your everyday speech. What it does mean, however, is developing a well-rounded vocabulary and knowing how and when to use even the simplest words correctly as you communicate.

Many people commonly confuse everyday words, mispronounce them, or misuse them in sentences because they don't know the true meaning of the words. To begin to develop a stronger vocabulary, you need to properly incorporate new words into your everyday speech (and writing) in order to benefit from them.

There are many ways to enhance your vocabulary. Simply reading books is one excellent strategy that will help you over time. You can also study the dictionary. A more immediate solution, however, is to participate in a self-paced course, such as Verbal Advantage, which is designed to enhance your vocabulary and insure you are properly able to use the new words you learn as you enhance your vocabulary to a college graduate or post-graduate level.

Tim Dunham is the inbound telemarketing manager at Word Success, LLC, the company which markets the popular Verbal Advantage audio vocabulary-building course (*www.verbaladvantage.com*), which has been successfully used by more than 200,000 people throughout the world.

According to Dunham, "Verbal Advantage is a listen and learn course. It teaches the 3,500 most commonly misused words in the English language. It starts out at a college entry level and proceeds progressively to a Ph.D. level. During the course, students learn each word's pronunciation and definition, as well as antonyms and synonyms. Colorful examples are used to help students learn how to use each word in its proper context, which is very important."

To insure the student's success, Verbal Advantage teaches vocabulary in groups of 10 words at a time, so it's divided into easy lessons that take between 15 and 30 minutes each to complete. "In addition to teaching vocabulary, Verbal Advantage teaches students to improve their writing skills; reading retention; verbal skills and their ability to listen to other individuals whom they're talking to, so that they are able to adjust their vocabulary to another individual," adds Dunham.

As a telemarketer or telesales professional, the people you come into contact with, including your prospects, customers, coworkers, and superiors, will all judge you by the words you use to communicate. Being able to articulate and be precise and having the ability to control conversation flow are all imperative for someone who makes a living communicating over the telephone. Dunham explained that the ability to mirror the person you're talking to, in terms of your vocabulary level, is also an important skill to develop. To do this successfully, you, as the telesales professional, must develop excellent listening skills as well as top-notch verbal skills. "You need to hear what your prospects and customers are saying and respond accordingly," says Dunham. "If someone has a vast array of words at their disposal, they can more easily communicate and convey their sales message when they're engaged in telesales."

Simply improving your vocabulary is not a guaranteed method for immediately boosting your sales or earning a raise, but it is a valuable skill that you can easily incorporate with your other professional skills (described in Chapter 9) in order to become a better communicator and a more highly skilled telesales professional. By constantly improving upon your professional skill set and honing your telephone sales skills, you will see ongoing improvement in your ability to close sales, generate larger sales, and more easily retain your customers.

As you develop your sales pitch, incorporate words that convey meaning, emotion, and power. Keep in mind that there are many ways to present the same material. For each prospect or customer, you will most likely need to customize or adapt your pitch so the person you're selling to can more easily relate. No matter what, however, because you're relying on words to sell your product or service, make sure you choose words that grab attention and are descriptive.

Adjectives and descriptive phrases can be powerful sales tools as you promote your product/service and its benefits. For example, you could say, "You will save when you buy our product." Using more powerful words, however, here are some ways that same concept could be rephrased:

- ◆ "You will experience monumental savings when you buy our product."
- ◆ "By taking advantage of our product, you will experience substantial savings."
- ◆ "Your company will immediately benefit from spectacular savings when you buy our product."

Which of these sentences sounds more appealing? As you create the script for your pitch, take full advantage of a thesaurus. (If you're using Microsoft Word, a thesaurus is built in.

Under the "Tools" pull-down menu, select "Language" and then select "Thesaurus.") To describe the large size of something, words such as *big* convey an idea, but more powerful words are *monumental, substantial, immense, mammoth, colossal,* and *abundant.*

When choosing the wording you'll use, don't confuse words, and never use words you don't know the meaning of because you think that will make you sound more intelligent. In the English language, there are many words that are commonly confused or misused. For example, *beside* means alongside, but *besides* means also. An *allusion* is a reference to something, an *illusion* is a false image, and a *delusion* is a false belief. Make sure you know the points you're trying to make and then select the correct words to convey those points.

Remember that big and obscure words aren't usually the best words to use in a sales pitch. While always remaining professional, it's always best to stick with language that's simple, easy to understand, and believable. Try to eliminate lazy speech patterns, such as "um," "yeah," and "ya know," which can convey nervousness or sloppy use of the language.

Finally, when communicating with others, use the word that will capture your prospect's attention and that he or she most likes to hear: his or her name! Incorporate someone's name into your conversation by making comments such as:

- ◆ "John, let me tell you about...."
- ◆ "John, that's an excellent point...."
- ◆ "John, have you ever thought about...?"
- ◆ "John, please let me take a moment of your time to...."

Pronunciation

As important as it is to sound intelligent using the proper vocabulary to make your point in an interesting and exciting way, make sure that you're properly pronouncing the words you use. How good your pronunciation is will have a direct impact on your ability to be understood by the person you're speaking with.

Incorrectly saying a word can be as damaging as misusing a word. Especially if you're reading a telemarketing script, make sure you properly pronounce each word. Make a point to pronounce the vowels in each word to enhance your ability to be understood, don't run words together when you speak, and don't leave out syllables. If you find yourself stumbling on a word or hesitating when using it, find a synonym for that word that's easier to say in the context you're using it.

Depending on where you're from or what your background is, perhaps you speak with some type of accent. Learning how to control or even get rid of your accent can be helpful when telemarketing, because it's vital that people be able to understand you and relate to what you're saying. After all, people tend to relate best to those who are most like themselves. If you're communicating with an accent to someone without an accent, it builds a potential barrier between you and the prospect.

Speed of Delivery

People normally speak at a rate of less than 60 words per minute. When people are uncomfortable or nervous, however, their rate of speaking can increase dramatically. During your telemarketing activities, especially if you're reading a script, it's important to speak at a normal rate—not too fast (making you sound nervous) and not too slow (making it sound as though you're having trouble reading the script or understanding what you're saying). The best way to gauge your speech rate is to record yourself during a presentation or sales pitch and then go back and critique it. Does it sound as if you're holding a normal, everyday conversation or that you're speaking too fast in order to convey as much information as possible before the prospect hangs up on you? It should never sound as though you're reading (even if you are following a script word for word) when engaged in telemarketing efforts.

Some people naturally speak quickly, whereas others speak more slowly. Once you know what your own normal speech rate is, you may need to consciously adapt it slightly to accommodate the person you're speaking with. In addition to altering your speech pattern, make an effort to adjust your vocabulary to cater to the person you're speaking with. You don't want to alienate your prospect using words, phrases, or concepts that aren't readily understood or to present your pitch in a manner that goes over the prospect's head. Although it's important to sound extremely knowledgeable and credible, it's equally important to be perceived as an equal from an intellectual standpoint.

Conveying Emotions

Throughout this book, the importance of conveying positive emotions when you speak on the phone has been repeated. Imagine how boring it would be to receive a phone call from a telesales professional and listen to a three-, five-, or 10-minute pitch given by someone with a monotone voice that conveys no joy, excitement, or emotion. Would you stay on the line? Probably not!

Simply by adjusting the mood or emotion you convey, the meaning of what you're saying and the impact it has on someone could change dramatically. Likewise, the emotions you convey reflect on who you are as a person and help the person you're speaking with create an impression about you early on.

Because the only things the person you're speaking with has to work with in terms of formulating his or her impression during a telephone call is what you say and how you say it, it's important to add as much emotional impact into what you're saying as possible so that you're perceived to be friendly, out-going, sincere, and intelligent.

Whenever you're trying to sell anything over the telephone, make sure the expression on your face properly conveys the emotion you're trying to communicate. You want your prospects to enjoy speaking with you, even if they're having a bad day. Using slight inflections in your voice, a sales pitch can sound totally sincere or as though you're trying to pull the wool over the prospect's eyes. If you genuinely sound as if you believe what you're saying, the person you're speaking with is more apt to believe it, too. Likewise, if it comes across as though you're just saying the words and don't necessarily believe them, you're giving the prospect ample reason not to believe what you say either.

Using Your Voice As A Sales Tool

The concept of mimicking the person you're speaking with is a highly useful tool if done correctly. First, you must understand and develop your own style of speaking. For example, do you tend to speak quickly? Do you adapt an upbeat and friendly tone when you speak, or are you more low-key and serious? Following are some words that describe someone's behavior when they speak. Which one(s) best describe you?

- Agreeable.
- Ambitious.
- Arrogant.
- Confident.
- Critical.
- Cryptic.
- Decisive.
- Disrespectful.
- Dominating.

- ♦ Dramatic.
- ♦ Emotional.
- ♦ Enthusiastic.
- ♦ Flaky.
- ♦ Persistent.
- ♦ Pushy.
- ♦ Respectful.
- ♦ Serious.
- ♦ Stuffy.
- ♦ Thoughtful.

Pick three to five words from this list (or add your own) that best describe your personal communication style when you speak.

1. _____
2. _____
3. _____
4. _____
5. _____

Once you know how you generally communicate, when you begin speaking with someone new during a call, for example, quickly evaluate his or her communication style and needs. If someone speaks slowly, chances are he or she will relate better to someone who also speaks slowly, so to achieve the most positive impact on that person you should bridge the gap between your two communication styles and try to be more like the person you're speaking with.

When using your voice to communicate, it's always best to be brief and to the point, especially when telemarketing. Try to be informative, entertaining, stimulating, and engaging, while at the same time, catering to the prospect or customer's needs, wants, hopes, and desires. Most importantly, send clear messages and seek out understanding. If necessary, ask questions such as, "Do you understand what I'm saying?" or "Does that make sense to you?"

Don't Just Speak, Listen!

Being an effective listener will help you gauge the buying mood of prospects, deal with their concerns, build relationships, and know when to begin closing a sale. Although it's easy to speak, present your sales pitch, and sell, many people find it particularly challenging to stop talking and listen to what their prospects and clients have to say. Any real conversation involves speaking and spending at least an equal amount of time listening to the other person, then responding properly to what's said.

When someone is listening to another person speak, his or her true comprehension of what's being said is only about 50 percent. It's possible for the brain to focus on a lot more information than what's actually being said, which is why it's easy for the listener's mind to wander. So, when you make your sales pitch, assume that only about half of what you're saying actually gets through to the prospect. Thus, repeating key points in different ways is always useful. Likewise, unless you put your own listening skills to full use, only about half of what the prospect says to you will be comprehended. If you're not listening carefully and being an active listener, important concerns or thoughts your prospect may have could easily go unaddressed, and that could mean losing a sale.

Developing excellent listening skills is important. As with anything else, it takes practice. When someone else is speaking, pay attention! Focus on the content or meaning of what's being said, not necessarily the other person's delivery. Also, don't allow yourself to get distracted by whatever is happening around you. Make sure you concentrate on what's being said, without interrupting the person who is speaking. Prepare yourself to follow up by reiterating or paraphrasing what was said to you and then addressing the situation. Restate, in your own words, what was just said. Don't simply repeat what the person said word for word. As you do this, focus only on the topic at hand—that is, the main idea or concept that was just conveyed to you.

Reiterating what was said demonstrates that you were not just listening, but that you understand what was said. It shows the prospect you care about him or her and that you understand what he or she is thinking. You're now in a much more credible position to address an issue and formulate an intelligent reply. This is an easy method for showing agreement or empathy with the person you're speaking with.

When someone is speaking, even if he or she is rambling, try to discern what point he or she is trying to make and focus in on that issue or thought. Even if what's being said is incorrect, offensive, or inappropriate, never allow your emotions to hamper your ability to process the information and then respond in a professional manner. It's normal human behavior to become defensive or dismissive when someone says things you don't agree with. As a telesales professional, when there is disagreement, you need to understand it, analyze it, and transform it into agreement so that you can make your sale. Tuning out or reacting emotionally won't allow you to do this.

It's totally appropriate to take a moment of silence (or a dramatic pause) and think about a response or what to say next in various situations, such as after asking a question, after being asked a question, after an important point has been made, or when emotions start getting out of control. A slight pause can add impact to what you're saying or can be used to give you a few seconds to clarify ideas in your head before responding inappropriately or with incorrect information.

If it's done correctly, being an active listener should take as much energy and attention as speaking, especially when you're engaged in selling. Make sure that your prospect or client feels comfortable speaking with you. There are many ways to do this, but to help make that person feel comfortable with voicing his or her opinions or asking questions, use statements such as, "John, that's an excellent point..." or "That's an interesting question, John...."

Throughout your sales pitch and when you're interacting with prospects or clients, encourage the other person to speak. Asking open-ended questions and soliciting ideas or opinions are excellent strategies for achieving this.

Sound-Checking Your Voice

During any sales pitch, evaluate your voice and make sure it's being used to its utmost advantage as a powerful sales tool. For example, ask yourself:

- Are you successfully communicating your message so that it's heard and understood by the prospect?
- Are you being descriptive enough in what you're saying and able to establish (perceived) need and create excitement about your product/service?
- Do you sound enthusiastic and knowledgeable about your company and its product/service?
- Are you speaking at an understandable speed, using pauses when appropriate, to communicate your message without mumbling?
- Are you conveying the proper emotions? Are you injecting a variation of tones and pitches into your voice to make yourself more enjoyable to listen to?

- ◆ Are you spending enough time listening to what your prospect has to say?
- ◆ Is all of your equipment (including your telephone headset) operating properly so that you can be clearly heard? (If the headset, for example, isn't set up correctly or the microphone isn't the proper distance from your mouth, the prospect might not be able to hear you.)

Mistakes To Avoid

In terms of how you use your voice when telemarketing, here are some of the common mistakes to avoid, based on information described within this chapter:

1. Control the volume of your voice so you don't speak too quietly or too loudly, causing you to inadvertently give the wrong impression about yourself.

2. The speed at which you speak should be the same as if you're holding an in-person conversation. It's common for people who are nervous, for example, to speak too quickly. This will hurt your credibility and impact your chance of someone listening to your sales pitch. Pace yourself.

3. Never use words you don't know the meaning of or that you think the person you're speaking with won't understand. If the words don't nicely flow in your conversation, don't use them.

4. Don't slur your words, drop syllables, or run words together when you speak. This makes it much harder for you to be understood.

5. Don't misuse or mispronounce words, as this can be detrimental to your credibility.

6. Avoid using words with meanings that could be misconstrued.

7. Never allow your personal mood to be conveyed in the tone of your voice or in the emotions you communicate over the telephone when speaking to prospects or clients. Even if you're having a bad day or you're depressed or angry, when engaged in telemarketing, the emotions you convey should be friendly, upbeat, sincere, and engaging. One of the worst mistakes you can make is to sound desperate to make a sale. It's perfectly acceptable to ask for the sale, but if your tone or actions make you seem too desperate, it could be a turn-off to the prospect.

8. Don't interrupt the person you're speaking with. If the prospect believes it's important to voice his or her concern, offer an opinion, or ask a question, what he or she has to say should be equally important to you, the salesperson. Never ignore or dismiss what someone has to say.

9. When trying to mirror your prospect or client, in terms of how he or she uses his or her voice, be subtle. You don't want your actions could be misinterpreted as insulting.

10. When acknowledging what someone has to say or responding to a question, for example, you want to repeat what the other person says in order to demonstrate your understanding. However, avoid the common mistake of simply reciting what was just said word for word.

11. As part of your sales pitch, you run the risk of confusing your prospect/customer if you overuse industry buzzwords or too much technical jargon. Make sure you gauge the level of knowledge of

your prospect before using technical terms that might not be understood. Using a bunch of buzzwords and technical terms won't automatically make you (the telemarketer) sound more intelligent.

12. Never use a speakerphone when making any type of sales call. In addition to poor sound quality, this creates greater perceived distance and a potential distraction between you and the prospect.

It will ultimately be a need or desire for the product or service you're selling that will impact the buying decisions of your prospects, but how well you present your sales pitch and communicate with the people you're trying to sell to will definitely impact your success. Now that you've determined the perfect target market for your product/service, developed your sales message, adopted the proper attitude, and learned some of the secrets of using your voice as a powerful sales tool, in the next chapter, you will put all of the steps together as the entire step-by-step telemarketing process is explained—from preparing for each call to ultimately closing the sale and building up a long-term relationship with your customers.

Chapter 7

THE
TELEMARKETER'S
AGENDA

E very telemarketer and telesales professional has an agenda. As you develop your own agenda, it's important to first look at the big picture—the long-term. When considering this, your overall telemarketing agenda should be to sell your product or service successfully using the telephone and to help solve the problems or fill the needs of your customers and clients.

For each call you make, however, you must also have a short-term agenda. This agenda should be to carefully follow each step in the telesales process and insure that you pay careful attention to details.

This chapter focuses on developing your short-term agenda for each outbound sales call you make. It will walk you through each step in the telemarketing process once you're actually ready to begin making calls. Thus far in *Top Telemarketing Techniques*, each element in the telemarketing process has been broken up and explained. Now, these elements are put back together and placed into a logical order so you will better understand the sales cycles, which is the process telemarketers go through with each and every call they make.

Based on the product or service you'll be selling, your own telemarketing agenda may vary slightly, so as you read this chapter, begin to formulate your own customized agenda to meet your needs. As you'll see, some of the steps described here have already been focused upon elsewhere in this book. Now you can put that information into perspective as you look at the bigger picture.

What you're about to read are the 16 steps you'll go through for each and every outbound sales call you make. If you'll be doing inbound telemarketing, several of these steps don't apply. By the time you're ready to follow these steps, you should already know what product/service you're selling and have developed a sales pitch. (Chapter 4, Chapter 8, and Chapter 10 will help you create and fine-tune your sales script. If you're having trouble writing your own telemarketing script, consider hiring a professional scriptwriter. Chapter 10 offers a list of several companies that specialize in script writing for inbound or outbound telemarketing.)

Step 1

Determine the People Who/Companies That Will Buy Your Product/Service

Before you can begin making calls to sell your product or service, learn everything you possibly can about what you are selling. In addition, you'll find it much easier to sell a product/service if it's something you truly believe in. Part of learning about your product/service involves developing a detailed understanding of who your target customer is, why they need your product/service, how your product/service will be used by the target customer, and what problem or need you'll be filling by selling your target customer your product/service.

As you consider your target audience, focus on their specific characteristics, needs, desires, and buying habits. Customize your sales pitch so that it caters to your target customers. (Chapter 4 focuses on determining your target audience and developing the perfect sales message for your product/service.)

If you're selling directly to customers, focus on the demographics of those consumers to better target them. As you define your target audience, consider their sex, age group, income level, marital status, geographic area, buying habits, career, ethnic background, or any other pieces of data that might better help you define, find, and target your ideal customer.

When you're selling to businesses, you also want to define your target customer by focusing such factors as what business the prospect is in, its industry, its size, its geographic area, or its annual sales, for example. The more you know about your intended customers, the easier it will be to understand their needs and wants as you make your sales pitch.

Step 2

Prospecting

Once you have defined your target customer, the next step is to locate those individuals or companies and put together your prospect or lead list. To save you time, resources, money, and energy as you actually begin making your calls, it's always better to invest your time and money in developing your prospect or lead list to insure the following:

- ◆ The prospects on the list represent your target customers.
- ◆ The information on your list is timely and accurate. If you have a 30-percent inaccuracy rate within your list (which is common), when you begin making calls, 30 percent of your time will

be wasted tracking down and contacting bad leads. Remember: The more accurate your list is, the fewer calls you need to make in order to reach the decision-maker.

♦ You have the appropriate buyer's name as well as his or her phone number. Especially when selling to companies, once you pinpoint the company you'll be targeting, it's important to focus your selling efforts on the right person: the decision-maker. Making your sales pitch to anyone else will waste everyone's time. If you can't obtain the name of the buyer through your preliminary research (when selling to companies), at least pinpoint the job title of the person who makes the buying decisions for what you're selling.

♦ The prospects you will be contacting can afford to purchase your product/service. If the people you're selling to can't afford it, there's no point in targeting them as prospects.

♦ You know your prospect's business cycle and when they're most apt to purchase what you're selling.

As you're developing your prospect or lead list, take a look at your key competitors and ask yourself who their customers are. Who is using their product/service and how is your competitor successfully reaching its target audience? If you choose to pursue the customers of your competitors, one of your additional goals will be to convince those people or companies to switch to your product/service. Thus, part of your sales pitch must also now include all of the benefits, perks, and cost savings, for example, that you offer over your competitors.

In addition to examining your competitors, to develop your own lead list, think about other places you're most apt to find information and contacts that fit within your target audience. For example, you might contact a list broker (a company that sells lists of names/prospects) that can be customized to a telemarketer's needs (see Chapter 13 for more information about list brokers). You may discover that buying or renting the subscription list from a magazine, newspaper, or newsletter is appropriate, or that the mailing list from a particular industry association will contain the perfect prospects. The telephone book, public records, industry directories, and other sources of data can also be useful when compiling your own lead/prospect list.

Step 3

Prioritize Your Target Accounts

Once you've developed your prospect or lead list, analyze it carefully. If necessary, do some additional research about those individuals or companies so that when you begin making calls you'll know as much as possible about the people you're calling. Armed with some knowledge about your target customer, you should be able to review your prospect list and pick out the individual names (particularly if you're selling to companies) that are most apt to buy what you're selling. If you're targeting consumers, their demographic data will obviously be more useful than their name when making this determination.

Go through your prospect list, before you start making calls, and pick out those leads that are most apt to buy your product/service and kick off your telemarketing efforts by contacting those most qualified leads. This selection process may be slightly subjective. As you pick up the phone, you want to know that the people or companies you're calling have been somewhat prequalified. Thus, instead of making "cold calls" to total strangers, in reality, you're making "warm calls" to strangers you know have a definite want or need for your product/service.

Step 4

New Business Development

Telemarketing can be used in many ways by companies to increase sales and improve customer service. In addition to using cold calls (or warm calls) to generate new business from prospects you've never before contacted and who know little or nothing about your company, you can also use telemarketing to obtain repeat business from existing customers and/or to enhance your relationship with customers you've done business with in the past.

Telemarketing is a highly effective tool for generating new or additional revenue, but as you make the calls and allocate your resources to a telesales effort, you need to carefully define what your objectives are. Are you looking to gain new customers? Generate new business from existing customers? Convince your competitor's customers to switch to your product/ service? Each of these objectives will require a totally different sales pitch and approach as you begin making calls. In terms of your own business's objectives, consider how telemarketing can be used for new business development and create an appropriate game plan.

Step 5

Prepare For Each Call

As you're sitting at your desk, staring at the phone and preparing to dial your first prospects, it's important to first properly prepare for each call. This preparation includes:

- ◆ Making sure you're in the right mindset and have the right attitude (see Chapter 5).

- Having your sales script, notes about your product/ service, and information about each of your prospects in front of you.

- Having information about what your competition is offering and being prepared to convince the prospect about the benefits of what you're selling.

- Having a clearly defined goal in terms of what you are trying to accomplish with the specific call you're about to make. For example, is the goal to prequalify a prospect and set up an in-person appointment; make a sale over the telephone; or generate interest and then follow up by sending catalogs, a proposal, or other information?

- Creating the perfect telemarketing environment for you to perform well in. Make sure you will be able to focus 100 percent of your attention on the prospect or customer you're calling. Eliminate any possible distractions. If necessary, close and lock your office door and/or instruct your secretary to hold all incoming calls.

- Make sure your telephone headset is connected to the phone and working properly (if you'll be using one).

Step 6

Dial for Dollars: Make the Call

Through experience, based on what you're selling, you'll discover that every call you make will follow a specific sales cycle, which includes getting past the gatekeeper (secretary, receptionist, and so forth), getting the decision-maker on the phone, making your sales pitch, handling objections, closing the sale, and doing the necessary follow-up work. You'll also learn that the majority of calls you make, no matter how good your lead list is, will result in rejection or not getting through to the proper decision-maker. Telemarketing is a numbers game. Elsewhere in this book, you'll read plenty of strategies for overcoming objections, getting through to the right person and how to track your success.

As you call each of your prospects, one of three things will happen:

1. You'll reach a gatekeeper. This can be a secretary, receptionist, company operator, or the assistant to the person you're trying to reach. Your immediate goal is to get past this gatekeeper so you can talk directly with the decision-maker. If you're not sure who the decision-maker is, you'll need to gather information from the gatekeeper by asking questions. (See Step 7 in this chapter.)

2. You'll reach the decision-maker's voice mail. Depending on the situation, you'll probably want to leave a message that's upbeat and that compels the prospect to call you back. Try to create some urgency in your message and repeat your name and phone number twice, to insure the person listening to your message will get it. If you work for an employment agency and you're calling a client to inform him or her about an applicant you think would be perfect for the prospect to hire, your voice mail message might go something like this:

   "Hello, Mr. Smith. This is Ellen Bendremer from XYZ Employment Agency. I am calling because I understand you may be looking to hire a new executive assistant. A resume recently crossed my desk from an applicant I believe would be perfect for your opening. She has six years of related experience working for one of your competitors and her references are extremely impressive. Please give me a call a back as soon as possible, so we can chat about this applicant. You can reach me at (617) 555–1234. Again, this is Ellen Bendremer from XYZ Employment Agency and you can reach me at (617) 555–1234."

If, after you leave a voice mail, you don't get a response, you'll definitely want to call back, this time during a different time of the day. When you're having trouble reaching a particular person, sometimes it's best to call before or after the normal business day. This is when the gatekeepers are not on the job but when executives, who tend to get to work early and stay late, are most apt to answer their own phones.

It's important that when you leave a second or a third voice mail message, you come across as persistent but not annoying. Make sure enough time has passed in between each call. With each message, you'll want to take a creative approach in order to capture the prospect's interest. For example, on a third message, you might state, "I've tried to reach you a few times to tell you about (insert a brief description of your product/service). If you are not the best person I should be speaking with, could you please give me a call with the appropriate contact person's name and phone number..."

3. You will get through to the appropriate decision-maker and be able to make your sales pitch. (See Step 8 in this chapter.)

Step 7

Handle Gatekeepers

In many cases, getting through the gatekeeper is your first big challenge in any telesales call. A gatekeeper can be a secretary, receptionist, personal assistant, or anyone who answers the phone and makes the decision about how to route your call. There are many different strategies for accomplishing this (some of which are described within Chapter 11). Ultimately, you'll want to discover a few strategies that work well for you personally, based on your own personality and style and what you're selling. (In Chapter 14, you'll read an interview with telemarketing expert Barry Maher, who is president of Barry Maher & Associates. His best strategy for getting past the gatekeeper is to take the simple and direct approach. He asks for the person by their first name, as if he already knows the person and expects to be connected to him or her. For example, he might say to the gatekeeper, "Hi, this is Barry. I'm calling for Bob.")

Whatever approach you take when dealing with gate-keepers, always be professional and friendly. After all, gatekeepers have the power to provide you with information and get you on the phone with the person you need to speak with. Often, they also handle the decision-maker's schedule and determine which calls get through and what appointments get made. These people also have the power to keep you from getting connected to the appropriate person.

Don't be afraid to ask fact-finding questions when speaking with gatekeepers and to ask for their help. Explain who you are and why you're calling, then ask for the name of the best person to speak with. You might also ask if the gatekeeper knows when the best time to reach the decision-maker would be (assuming he or she isn't currently available).

Step 8

Make Contact and Talk with the Decision-maker

Okay, you've done your homework, you've gotten past the gatekeeper, and now you hear that all-important "hello" from the decision-maker. What you say and how you conduct yourself during the next few seconds are critical. You can either capture the decision-maker's attention and keep them on the phone long enough to make your pitch, or you could receive instant rejection and be hung up on.

The best introduction is a straightforward one. Briefly introduce yourself and the company your represent, then ask the prospect if he or she has a moment to talk. Making calls is a top priority in your day, but there's a good chance you're interrupting the person you're calling, so show respect. Based on the prospect's reactions in the first few seconds of the call, try to ascertain his or her personality type and learn as much as you can about this person, so you can custom tailor your pitch to meet his or her needs.

Next, use the one- or two-sentence sales line that's a key attention-grabber in your script. It's designed to capture the attention of the prospect and keep him or her listening. This line should summarize who you are and what you do. At this point, you might receive one of the following objections:

- ◆ If someone abruptly states, "I'm not interested" politely ask, "What is it you're not interested in?" Use the answer to keep him or her on the phone and continue your pitch.

- ◆ If the prospect says, "Send me information," respond by asking, "What type of information can I provide you with to help you make an informed decision?"

- ◆ If someone states, "I'm busy and can't talk right now," ask when a better time would be for you to call back. Try to set a define telephone appointment, then quickly restate the benefit you're offering.

Once you've introduced yourself, stated why you're calling, and determined the prospect is willing to listen to what you have to say, verify that you are, in fact, talking to the appropriate decision-maker. Assuming you are, present your sales pitch. (See Step 9.)

Step 9

Present Your Sales Pitch

As you already learned in Chapter 4, having the right sales message and presentation is critical. Your objective is to communicate information about your product or service so that everything you say somehow addresses the needs or wants of the prospect or somehow helps to solve a problem the prospect is facing. Focus on the benefits of what you're offering.

Part of your sales pitch should also involve asking open-ended questions so you have the opportunity to learn more about your prospect and his or her needs. You want to demonstrate that what you're offering is a perfect match for those needs. To help you do this, you'll want to work toward developing a relationship with the prospect. This can be done in many ways—for example, by building upon things you have in common on a personal level.

At the same time you're selling your product or service to the prospect and gathering information that will help you make that sale, you want to continue to utilize the information you gather in order to continue to qualify him or her. You need to know the prospect needs the product/service and has the money to pay for it, and that you're dealing with the right person or people who make the buying decision. Once you know this is the case, part of your objective is to convince the prospect of this and to obtain his or her agreement.

Step 10

Trial Close

Once you've demonstrated the solutions you have to offer and have obtained agreement from the prospect that what you're selling is needed, experiment with a trial close. If this works, great—you just made a sale. If the trial close doesn't work, it will allow you to pinpoint any additional objections the prospect has and address them. At this point, you want to isolate and focus on each objection and overcome it before attempting to close the sale again. (Chapter 8 and Chapter 10 demonstrate how to best utilize trial closes in your sales pitch and discuss how and when they're appropriate to use.)

Step 11

Deal With and Overcome all Objections

You won't always have to ask questions in order to determine what the prospect's objections are. Without being prompted, he or she will often voice their own questions, opinions, and concerns during your pitch. Aside from the obvious objections, that are often money- or price-related, there will be a handful of other common objections that will come up repeatedly based on what you're selling. For each of these objections, plan in advance how you'll deal with them and be prepared to work directly with each prospect to overcome their objections—one at a time.

During this process, follow these basic steps:

1. Identify each objection.
2. Develop an understanding of the objection; ask questions.
3. Demonstrate an understanding of each objection by repeating it back to your prospect in your own words.
4. Empathize with the prospect.
5. Offer a solution to the objection.
6. Obtain agreement with the prospect.
7. Move on to the next objection or try to close the sale.

At some point in your pitch, in between presenting your solution(s) and going for the close, you'll need to discuss money. Before the cost of your product or service comes up, however, you'll be in a much stronger position if the prospect already agrees they have a want or need for what you're offering.

When discussing price, there are again several strategies you can incorporate, based on your personal preferences and what you're selling. One approach is to say something along the lines of, "And here's the good news...." before stating the price, implying that what you're offering is affordable or even a bargain based on what the prospect is getting. (Telemarketing expert Barry Maher discusses one of his favorite approaches for discussing price within Chapter 14.)

Whether you're offering your product or service at a highly competitive price or what you're offering is priced at a premium, it's always a good strategy to have multiple options available for the prospect. Start off by trying to sell the most expensive option or plan. If you receive a rejection (due to the prospect's inability to afford what you're offering), drop to the next lesser-expensive option. For example, if you're selling a subscription-based product or service, start off by trying to sell a five-year contract. If that doesn't work, try for a three-year contract. Instead of losing a sale, be prepared to offer a two-year or even a one-year contract. Only offer a less expensive option when it's clear the prospect is absolutely rejecting what you've offered thus far, and the main objection is price. You can also negotiate by offering a prepayment discount, a cash discount, a payment plan, or some other model for compensation.

After addressing each of the issues or objections, try another trial close and keep repeating this process until you either close a sale or it becomes clear there is no sale to be made.

Step 12

The Close

Whether you're involved with inbound or outbound telemarketing, the most important aspect of the call is the close. This is the stage of a call that directly leads to the sale. (Chapter 8 focuses exclusively on closing sales and talks about some of the many different strategies you can use to accomplish this.)

In terms of your telemarketing, closing might not necessarily mean making a sale. The goal of your call might be to set up an in-person appointment or get the prospect to request additional information. Your close refers to achieving the objective of the call or, at the very least, moving that prospect further along the sales cycles as you work toward closing the sale.

The object of the close is to obtain commitment from the prospect and to transform that prospect into a paying customer. You, as the salesperson, will often have to come right out and ask the prospect to buy what you're offering, even if you've already convinced him or her that it's needed. One of the biggest reasons why a telesales professional loses a sale is because he or she didn't close properly, even though the rest of the sales pitch, as well as the sales message and his or her attitude, were all on-target.

If the prospect agrees to buy your product/service, see if payment can be taken over the telephone using a credit card (if applicable). If not, make arrangements to get the contract or sales agreement signed, then arrange for payment(s) to be made in a timely manner.

Keep in mind that once you get a prospect to become a customer, be sure to take advantage of any up-sell opportunities that might exist either right away or in the near future. By up-selling, you can encourage a customer to purchase related products/services, additional options, accessories, or anything else that could increase the value of the sale and improve your ability to address the needs of your customer.

Step 13

End the Call

Whether or not you're able to close a sale during a call, there will be a point when the call needs to come to an end. Hopefully, you'll be able to do this by thanking the customer for his or her order and telling the customer how much you appreciate his or her business. Either way, make it clear that you're looking forward to a long-term relationship as the call draws to a close.

Use this closure to conclude any unfinished business, review the key points of the conversation (or the sale) with the prospect or customer, and then discuss what the next step will be. For example, if you just closed a sale, state that you will be delivering or faxing the related contract shortly and that you will call back to review it. Set a convenient time for this call. You can also use this time to review how your product or service can be implemented by the new customer and talk about what happens next. For example, you may need to arrange for an installer to visit the new customer or arrange for your product(s) to be delivered.

Finally, before saying goodbye, make sure the customer knows how to get in contract with you. Leave your name and phone number. You'll also want to enclose your business card or your contact information within any written correspondence. When you do ultimately say goodbye, make sure it's on a positive note, whether or not you closed a sale. The person you were on the phone with should leave the conversation having enjoyed speaking with you.

Step 14

Post-Call Wrap-up and Follow-through

The first thing you need to do upon hanging up the phone is write down detailed notes about the call, while the information is still fresh in your mind. Keep track of the date, the time, whom you spoke with, what was discussed, and what follow-up actions need to be taken. Enter this information within your prospect/lead database.

Whenever follow-up action needs to be taken on your part, make sure it's done in a very timely manner, whether it's faxing or sending additional information, creating a proposal, or making a follow-up call at a predefined time.

If you just made a sale, immediately complete the necessary paperwork, in terms of the contract, sales agreement, and so forth, and have that paperwork delivered to your prospect immediately via fax, messenger service, or overnight courier (such as FedEx). If you're dealing with a company, it may be necessary to obtain their purchase order. All of this should be done in a very timely manner, because you want the customer's signature on the contract before he or she has a chance to change his or her mind.

Step 15

Value-Added Services

Once you have transformed a prospect into a paying customer, it's important to stay in contact with that customer and build your relationship. One way to do this is to offer value-added services. Provide support helping the customer implement your product/service, make yourself available to answer questions, and make periodic follow-up calls to see how the prospect is doing. Anything you can do to improve your relationships with your customers will ultimately help you land future sales, develop repeat customers, and obtain word-of-mouth referrals from the people you do business with.

Step 16

Seek Out Referrals

It's always beneficial to you as the telemarketer to ask for referrals or new sales leads. Depending on the type of product/service you're selling and whom you're selling to, a prospect might suggest you call a relative or friend or one of the business's subsidiaries or other divisions.

One appropriate time to ask for a referral is after it becomes clear that the prospect you're speaking with isn't interested in what you're offering. At this point, instead of simply ending the call, you can ask, "Who do you know that may benefit from what I'm offering?"

Another appropriate time to ask for a referral is after you've established a strong working relationship with a customer. If that customer is happy with his or her relationship with you, he or she will often be happy to recommend you to friends, associates, coworkers, and so on.

Incorporating Visuals Into Your Sales Pitch

One common way to incorporate visuals into your sales pitch is to make sure the prospect receives your sales literature in advance of your call. Then, as you make your presentation, you can refer directly to those materials.

When you're selling a high-ticket item or making a somewhat technical sales pitch, an alternative technique is to incorporate a computer-based graphic presentation, such as one created using Microsoft PowerPoint, into the pitch. This is done by creating a specialized Website containing your graphic presentation. As you're making your telephone sales pitch, you can invite the prospect to visit your Website and view your visuals (such as photographs, charts, graphs, and bulleted lists). This technique can add a tremendous amount of impact to your overall sales pitch, yet it costs very little. Alternatively, you can e-mail a presentation, literature, or a specific proposal before, during, or after your sales call.

Chapter 8

CLOSING
THE SALE

Whatever business you're in, you're undoubtedly looking to increase sales. Perhaps you've decided to use telemarketing as a way of reaching new customers to generate business or contact existing customers to increase business. Making a top-notch sales presentation is, of course, important. But unless you're able to successfully transform a prospect into a customer by closing a sale, your telesales efforts will be in vain.

Closing a sale is a skill. It involves carefully evaluating your prospect, listening to their verbal reactions to your pitch, asking questions, and listening for nonverbal clues regarding their interest in your product/service. Just as there are countless ways to make an effective sales pitch and present your marketing message to your prospects, there are many techniques you can successfully incorporate to close a sale. After all, you need to come across as confident and at ease during your sales pitch, and the closing technique(s) you use should be an extension of that well-planned and rehearsed pitch.

This chapter focuses on the importance of closing a sale. Depending on the goal of your telemarketing efforts, the objective of your close may be to obtain a sale right on the spot (by taking an order, collecting payment information, and so forth). Your objective may, however, be to gather enough information from the prospect in order to qualify him or her and send literature to him or her, or it may be to set an in-person sales appointment. The closing techniques you use should allow you to achieve your objective and seal the deal.

Closing Begins Right at the Start

During each and every call you make, what you say, how you present what you're selling, and how you respond to questions should all be geared toward closing a sale. This process begins at the start of a call, when you're prequalifying the prospect, making sure you're making your presentation to the proper decision-maker, and learning about the prospect's needs.

Before actively initiating a closing strategy, however, insure you have all of the proper information. Determine that you're selling to the key decision-maker. During this process, you want to discover what the prospect's possible timeline is for making a decision, who is involved in the decision-making process, what the prospect's buying habits are, and what steps need to be taken to secure a sale. By asking questions and determining the prospect's needs, you'll be better equipped to make a convincing presentation. Armed with the proper information from each prospect, you can custom tailor your closing techniques to insure greater success.

Be on the Lookout for Buying Signals

As you already know, every telemarketing call you make will follow a pattern, which includes prequalifying the person you're speaking with, making your pitch, dealing with objections, and ultimately closing the sale. During each moment of every call, however, as a skilled telesales professional, be on the lookout for the prospect's buying signals.

A buying signal is some type of direct or subtle indication by the person you're speaking with that he or she has an interest in what you're selling. Rarely will a prospect simply state, "Okay, where do I sign? I want to buy your product!" in the middle of your pitch. Typically, you'll receive more subtle cues pertaining to the prospect's interest.

First and foremost, after making your initial introduction and explaining to the prospect why you're calling, if the person stays on the telephone to continue hearing what you have to say, that's a subtle buying signal, because it demonstrates an initial interest. During the sales pitch, a buying signal might be a positive comment, such as, "Really?"; "It can do that?"; or "That's very interesting!" as a result of you describing the key selling points or features of what you're selling.

When a prospect asks a positive question, that, too, should be considered a buying signal and be dealt with accordingly. For example, as you're making your presentation, if the prospect asks about price or financing, that's a clear indication you've captured his or her interest. More subtle questions might arise, such as, "Does your product come in blue?"; "If I place an order, how quickly can I expect shipment?"; or "Is there some type of discount if I buy in quantity?" These types of questions are all direct indicators that the prospect has an interest in what you're selling. It's your job to identify and build on this interest.

The Trial Close

There should be several points in your sales pitch where, once you've clearly obtained a certain level of interest, you put forth a trial close. Although a trial close could lead directly to a sale, it's more common to use this technique to measure the prospect's interest at various points during your sales pitch.

One trial close method involves obtaining ongoing agreement from the prospect. This can be done easily by asking a series of questions that will evoke a positive response or some form of agreement. As you make your pitch and offer information, you can ask questions such as, "Do you agree?"; "Does this make sense to you?"; "Are you with me?"; or "What do you think so far?" When you receive positive responses to several of these questions, it'll provide a clear indication that you're on the right track toward closing a sale.

When you receive a negative response, this is a symptom of a possible objection that needs to be properly addressed and dealt with. For example, if you ask, "Are you with me so far?" after describing several features of your product/service, and the prospect says, "No," you need to immediately backtrack, determine the cause of the confusion, and clarify it. As you lead up to the close, ideally, you want the prospect to have committed to a series of positive responses relating to what you're selling.

Depending on what you're selling, even if you get the proper decision-maker on the telephone, make your pitch, and generate a tremendous level of interest in and excitement about what you're offering, you won't always be able to close a sale on the first call. Even when it becomes clear that there's no immediate sale to be made, it's important to use trial closing techniques during that call in order to achieve some type of objective, even if that objective now involves scheduling another call, making an in-person presentation, or sending literature. Keep asking questions that will generate a positive response and work toward reaching agreement on as many issues as possible during each conversation. These issues might involve price, quantity, or shipment dates, for example. Each time you achieve agreement on a specific point or issue, you're one step closer to closing a sale.

Creating (Perceived) Value

One goal of your sales presentation should be to create value for what you're selling in the mind of the prospect. He or she needs to believe that what you're offering has value to him or her, is something he or she definitely needs, or is something he or she really wants. Your objective is to create the highest possible perceived value for your product/service by focusing on the features or benefits that the prospect will find most appealing, interesting, or useful. By creating a high-perceived value for what you're selling, you'll have fewer objections later when discussing price.

If what you're offering is not perceived as being valuable or needed by the prospect, your chances of closing a sale are slim to none. After all, how many people are willing to spend money on something they don't want or need? If, on the part of the prospect, there's risk involved in buying your product/service, it's also your responsibility to demonstrate clearly why it's necessary to take that risk and what the potential positive outcome will be.

Properly dealing with objections is an important part of any telemarketing call. When you're successful handling objections, you, as the salesperson, are in a much stronger position to close the sale. Thus, when an objection is brought up by the prospect, it's important to deal with it immediately and transform it into a positive, so you can once again achieve a level of agreement. For example, if someone brings up an objection about price, ask, "Is the price your only concern?" If he or she responds, "No," determine what his or her other concerns are so you can address each of them properly before continuing your pitch. If the response is, "Yes," you might ask, "If we agree on a price you're comfortable with, would you be interested in making a purchase today?" Once again, you're looking for commitment and agreement. Now, discuss the price and work harder to create perceived value of your product/service. Once this is done, ask for the order using a closing technique.

A Sampling of Closing Techniques

As you're about to discover, you can utilize many different types of closing techniques during a telesales call. Any of the techniques described here can be customized to better cater to the product/service you'll be selling. It's also an excellent strategy to learn from other telemarketing professionals with experience selling your product/service to determine which closing techniques they use successfully in various situations.

The "Would You Buy My Product?" Close

The closing technique you use can be extremely simple. After making your pitch, you can simply ask, "Why not give it a try?" or "Would you like to buy my product/service?" then wait for a response from the prospect. After directly asking for the sale, no matter how you word the question, you need to be quiet and wait for the prospect to respond. Speaking again, before the prospect responds, will often result in a lost or delayed sale. If the response to your question is favorable, close the sale immediately. If not, use this opportunity to discover the prospect's latest objection and deal with it.

The Ben Franklin Close

Another, slightly more detailed closing strategy involves describing all of the pros and each of the cons at the conclusion of your pitch. The pros should outweigh the cons, and the buy decision should become obvious to the prospect. It's sometimes a good idea to ask the prospect to grab a pad, draw two columns (one for pros and the other for cons), and have them list each on the paper as you're speaking with them on the phone.

The "Not Interested" Close

Not every call you make will result in a sale. One common response from the prospect will be, "I'm not interested." When you receive a comment similar to this, follow up immediately by asking, "Not interested in what?" and turn the tables. You could also make a comment such as, "A lot of my customers said they weren't interested at first. Let me take a moment to explain what changed their minds."

The Win-Win Close

Sometimes, a good closing technique for a situation involves allowing the prospect to choose between two win-win situations. Once you know there's interest, to get commitment for a sale, you could ask, "Would you prefer to receive delivery of the products tomorrow or on Friday?" or "Would you prefer the red model or the blue model?"

The Assumed Close

As the telemarketer, you'll sometimes discover that the best closing technique involves an assumed close. In this situation, you adopt the attitude that it's already a done deal and that you've made the sale, even though you haven't yet received a commitment from the prospect. For example, if you're selling advertising space in a newspaper, you could ask the prospect to start planning his or her ad by asking, "So, what would you want the ad to say?" or "Would next week or next month be the best time to start running your ad?"

Another variation of the assumed close is to make your pitch and then say, "Let's start getting the paperwork together. Who will be signing the agreement?" This is done before you actually receive a solid commitment from the prospect. Some people will go along with this technique and sign the papers. Others may not go along with your suggestion, so you may then need to isolate and overcome further objections before attempting to close the sale again.

The "Yes" Close

You've already learned the importance of obtaining agreement and commitment during your pitch. The "Yes" Close technique involves asking a series of questions you know you'll receive a "yes" answer to. After you've received multiple "yes" answers in a row, it becomes difficult for the prospect to say "no" to buying what you're selling, because he or she has already confirmed a need and/or want for it. For example, if you're selling advertising space in a newspaper, you could ask, "Do you agree that our publication will help you reach the customer's you're looking for?"; "Are you interested in making more sales and gaining more customers?"; "Do you understand that your ad could begin running immediately and that the customers will follow shortly thereafter?"; or "Do you agree this is a cost-effective advertising vehicle for your company?" Once you've received "yes" answers to these questions, when you ask the prospect to sign the contract and make a commitment, it becomes a logical decision for them.

The "Saving the Best for Last" Close

Price will often be a factor when it comes to making sales. One closing technique involves not discussing price until the very end of the pitch, and only once the prospect asks about it. During the pitch, if the prospect asks about price, that's a positive buying signal. Respond, however, by saying, "I'm saving the best for last. Let's see if we have a good match first." Then later, when you're ready to discuss price, ask, "If the price of my product/service makes sense, are you ready to move forward?" When he or she responds "yes," then discuss the price. If the prospect responds, "no," focus on the other issues and objections before talking about the price.

If someone says the price of what you're offering is too high, one response could be to ask, "Is the quality of what I'm offering not worth the price to you, or can you simply not afford what I'm offering?" Based on the response, you can modify your pitch accordingly.

Sometimes, how you deal with objections can directly result in a sale (or the loss of a sale). For example, once you peak the prospect's interest, but he or she makes a negative comment such as, "There's no way you could get me the units by Thursday!", you can turn this potential negativity into a positive buying signal by asking, "Suppose I could get you the units by Thursday. Would we have a deal?" Now you've turned a negative into a positive and received a potential commitment.

The Negotiated Close

Closing a sale often involves negotiation. The prospect might not be willing to buy exactly what you're selling, in the quantity you're selling it in, or at the price you're asking. When this becomes obvious, instead of losing the sale altogether, try using a trial offer to close the sale. Instead of offering your services for a one-year contract, for example, sell them a trial six-month contract. There will be times when compromises are required to close a sale. If, however, you prove the value of your product/service, the goal is to close the trial offer and then cultivate that customer by building a positive long-term relationship.

The "Don't Waste my Time" Close

After you've done your pitch, addressed the objections, and perhaps made multiple sales calls to the same prospect, you still might not be able to close the sale because the prospect is using various delay tactics. It may then become appropriate to make a comment such as, "I don't want to waste any more of your time or mine. Are you interested in buying my product/service or not?" Of course, this needs to be done in a friendly and professional way but, at the same time, you want to get the point across that you're looking for some type of decision.

Strategies to Assist the Close

No matter what type of closing technique you use, the following strategies will help insure your success:

- ◆ When closing any type of sale, it's important to constantly convey confidence and enthusiasm. During your sales pitch, and especially when you're working toward closing a sale, you never want to be wishy-washy or unsure of yourself.

- ◆ The techniques you use for the trial close and the regular close will be basically the same. The big difference between these two things is that a trial close involves making sure the prospect is with you along the way during the presentation, and the final close takes place after you've addressed all objections. Thus, a trial close can transform into a final close anytime a sale is made.

- ◆ Once you have agreement on an issue (or have overcome an objection), stop and go on to the next objection. Don't offer additional information that could backfire. If someone is ready to buy, stop selling and take the order. Don't oversell.

- ◆ When explaining something, especially if it's a complex or technical issue, don't ask, "Do you understand?" The prospect doesn't want to look stupid. Instead say, "I'm not sure I am explaining this very well. Am I making sense to you?" This puts the burden on you.

- ◆ If you started closing at the beginning and you've addressed all of the prospect's concerns, you're in the driver's seat. If there is any resistance, there is probably still some objection that needs to be dealt with.

- One common mistake telesales professionals make is waiting until the very end of the call to ask for a sale. If you do this, you have no clue why the prospect is saying "no" (if you receive a rejection). Thus, you have to go back and pinpoint the objection, then start from scratch. If you ask questions along the way, discover a need, and demonstrate how the product/service could fill a need, then get ongoing agreement, you'll have a much better chance of closing the deal. Don't just read a script. Interact with the prospect as much as possible before trying to close.

- Right from the start of any call, promote the value of your product/service. Never assume that the biggest objection the prospect will have is related to price. When telemarketers do this, they're often too anxious to offer discounts or other financial incentives when they may not be needed to close the sale. Remember that it's all about perceived value.

- It's important to understand that people don't like to be sold something, but they do like to make an intelligent buy. Your job is to assist the prospect in making an intelligent purchase and then to feel really good about it.

- Don't look at a rejection as a negative thing. Instead, try to learn from that rejection. Discover what you did wrong and how you can improve your pitch, starting with your next call.

- Remember to custom tailor your closing technique(s) to the prospect, based on the prospect's situation and personality. Don't just repeat something you've learned from this book. Close the deal based on a customized presentation for each of your individual prospects. Whenever possible, use a consultative approach to develop a stronger rapport.

- It's a common strategy to try to up-sell the prospect as soon as you close a sale. This technique can increase the value of the sale if done correctly, however, you never want to nickel-and-dime the new customer or add unnecessary pressure. Selling needed accessories, warrantees, or options can always be done at a later time. When to begin the up-sell process will depend on what you're offering, your relationship with the customer, his or her needs/wants, and his or her personality.

- Be on the lookout for broad or unclear phrases from the prospect and seek clarification. For example, if the prospect says, "This isn't exactly what we're looking for right now," ask what exactly he or she *is* looking for. If you get a response such as, "This looks pretty reasonable," ask, "What aspects seem reasonable and which don't?" When someone states, "Your price is not within our range?" respond by asking, "What is your range or budget?" Once you ask a question, be quiet and listen carefully to the response.

- One of the most important things telemarketers need to remember is that a sale is not closed until the paperwork has been signed and payment has been received. Thus, when you close a sale on the telephone, you either want to receive credit card payment on the spot or coordinate exactly how and when the contracts will be signed and payments will be made. Anytime someone agrees to buy what you're selling, you only have a short window of time to obtain the signatures on a contract and/or obtain payment. People's excitement about something new can wear off quickly. Take care of business immediately. When you get a commitment for a sale, don't make other sales calls right away. Instead, handle your paperwork and follow up immediately with the new customer.

Successful telemarketing is a process that involves incorporating a wide range of skills and techniques in order to achieve the desired results. Now that you have a basic understanding of what's involves in this whole process, you need to begin to perfect your own skills, incorporate your own knowledge and experiences, plus learn from the experiences of others. The next chapter focuses on how to perfect the skills you'll ultimately need to become a highly skilled and successful telesales professional.

Chapter 9

PERFECTING YOUR SKILLS

Talented telesales professionals are able to successfully harness and incorporate their skills, knowledge, experiences, and personal drive every time they're on the telephone dealing with a prospect or client. It's often a telemarketer's unique personal skill set, in addition to his or her knowledge of their product/service, that allows him or her to capture the attention of prospects and keep it long enough to make his or her pitch and close that all-important sale.

This chapter will help you analyze, tap, and ultimately enhance each of the skills you have or need in order to improve your talent as a telemarketer or telesales professional. Unfortunately, simply having a good skill set and a thorough knowledge of your product/service, for example, isn't enough. As you interact with clients and prospects, you need to know how and when to utilize the knowledge, skills, and experience you have to improve your chances of closing a sale.

The Skills Within Every Telemarketer's Arsenal

Anyone can dial a telephone, ask to speak with a specific person, and then read a prepared sales script (and hope that the script is good enough to generate a sale). Far fewer people, however, can take that script and work with it, interact with prospects and capture their attention, generate interest in a product/service, close a sale, and build a positive and long-lasting relationship with a customer. This, however, should be the goal of every telesales professional.

As with any job, having a solid, well-rounded education will provide you with the core knowledge you need, however, there are many skills that you might not have learned in school that, if utilized, can enhance your success as a telemarketer. Although all of the skills discussed here are important, it's impossible to measure how much any one of them will directly impact your ability to close sales. One of your goals should be to arm yourself with a well-rounded arsenal of skills that you can utilize to make yourself an overall better salesperson. The majority of these skills will help you excel not just in telemarketing, but in any job or career you choose to pursue.

Some of these additional skills include:

- Business writing skills.
- Vocabulary and proununciation.
- Public speaking and presentation skills.
- Negotiation and conflict resolution.
- Organization.
- Stress management.
- Time management.

Business Writing Skills

During the sales process, you'll often need to send information, follow up inquiries, and communicate with your prospect and clients in writing, either by mail, fax, or e-mail. Being able to generate well-written, informative, and concise business correspondence, contracts, and sales materials in a timely manner will vastly improve your credibility and ability to communicate properly with the people you do business with.

Having good written communication skills means knowing what to say and how to say it (using the correct words), plus being able to communicate thoughts, information, and ideas on paper. It also means utilizing proper spelling, punctuation, and formatting so you convey a highly professional image. After all, you could write an excellent business letter explaining all of the incredible reasons why someone should buy your product/service, but if that letter is full of spelling and grammatical errors or uses the wrong words to communicate your ideas, that letter will look as though it was written by an elementary school student, not a professional businessperson. This will dramatically tarnish your credibility and diminish your ability to properly communicate with prospects and clients.

The following are two short letters that might be included when sending a prospect your company's sales brochures. If you were the prospect, which of these letters would you take more seriously? Notice what's being said, the language used, the spelling, and the grammar.

Letter #1

January 15, 2003

Mr. John Smith
Vice president of Marketing
The ABC Company, Inc.
123 Main Street
Newyork, NY 10001

Dear Mr. Smith,

Thanks for talking with me on the fone today. You are a nice person. Here is the additional information you wanted. don't forget to call me if you have any questions. Our widgets are really, really good. They'll help your company lots. As you will see, we offer competitive prices and 15-years worth of knowledge and experience which your company could probably benefit from.

Sincerely,

John Doe

◆ ◆ ◆

Letter #2

January 15, 2003

Mr. John Smith
Vice President of Manufacturing
The ABC Company, Inc.
123 Main Street
New York, NY 10001

Dear Mr. Smith,

I enjoyed speaking with you this afternoon about all of the ways our newly designed widgets can be utilized in your manufacturing process to cut costs and improve output. Enclosed please find our latest product information, which outlines the many benefits of using our products and how my company's 15 years of exemplarily service to our customers will help The ABC Company better achieve its financial and sales goals.

Once you've reviewed the enclosed materials, I look forward to speaking with you again so that we can discuss, in greater detail, your specific needs and get you started with using our widgets immediately. I'll plan on giving you a call toward the middle of next week.

Thanks for much for your interest. I look forward to working with you in the near future.

Sincerely,

John Doe

◆ ◆ ◆

Learning to become a more proficient and eloquent writer when it comes to business correspondence will take time and practice, just as any other skills do. As you're developing these skills, take full advantage of using a word processor with a spelling and grammar checker, plus have someone else review and edit your letters before sending them. Even if you're an effective salesperson on the telephone, that image you've worked so hard to create with your prospects and customers needs to be demonstrated in every form of communication you have with them, including all of your letters, faxes, and e-mails.

In addition to a standard dictionary and thesaurus, many books and reference materials can help you become a more prolific business writer. A few excellent resources are: *Associated Press Stylebook and Libel Manual* (Addison-Wesley Publishing Company), *The Chicago Manual of Style: The Essential Guide for Writers, Editors, and Publishers* (The University of Chicago Press), *The Elements of Style* (Allyn & Bacon), and *The Elements of Business Writing: A Guide to Writing Clear, Concise Letters, Memos, Reports, Proposals, and Other Business Documents* (Longman).

Vocabulary and Pronunciation

The words you use and your ability to pronounce them correctly during a conversation will impact how you're perceived by your prospects. Using the wrong words or mispronouncing words can make you look less intelligent or ignorant. In addition to properly using words from the English language, chances are you'll need to utilize industry or product-specific buzzwords.

Chapter 6 offers detailed advice on how to use your voice, vocabulary, pronunciation, and diction as sales tools when communicating with prospects and customers on the telephone. By reading, taking additional classes, and/or listening to audio programs, for example, you can improve your vocabulary and use of the English language with relative ease, if you're willing to commit the time and energy to do so.

Public Speaking and Presentation Skills

Your public speaking skills will also prove extremely valuable when engaged in telemarketing. Although you may think of public speaking as communicating in-person before a group of people, many of the same skills apply to telemarketing, especially when engaged in a conference call with multiple decision-makers.

One of the best ways to enhance your public speaking and presentation skills is through practice. Once you have your sales script or presentation developed, you could always rehearse it over and over in front of a mirror or videotape yourself making a mock presentation in order to later critique your performance.

Another excellent way to develop and perfect these skills is by joining Toastmasters International ((949) 858–8255/ *www.toastmasters.org*), a nonprofit organization with chapters located throughout the world. Members work together, using proven methods, to learn how to speak more effectively. According to the organization, "At Toastmasters, members learn by speaking to groups and working with others in a supportive environment. A typical Toastmasters club is made up of 20 to 30 people who meet once a week for about an hour."

Each meeting gives everyone an opportunity to practice:

+ Conducting meetings.
+ Giving impromptu speeches.
+ Presenting prepared speeches.
+ Offering and receiving constructive evaluation.

Upon joining a Toastmasters club, each new member is given several manuals and other materials. Members also have access to a wide range of resources, such as books, audio and videocassettes on the topics of speaking and leading. To successfully make any type of in-person or telephone sales presentation using your public speaking skills, Toastmasters offers the following advice to help you prepare:

- ◆ Know the room. Be familiar with the room where you'll be speaking (if conducting your sales presentation in-person).

- ◆ Know the audience. Determine, in advance, who your audience is, what information they want to know, what they already know, and how the information you plan to present can help them.

- ◆ Know your material. Especially when it comes to sales, nothing is more important that having a thorough understanding of your product/service and a strong knowledge about your company. Not only do you need to be able to present information in an authoritative style, you must be able to answer questions intelligently.

- ◆ Relax. Your prospects and customers will be able to tell if you're overly anxious or nervous. If you know your material and you've rehearsed your presentation, you'll be able to more easily relax and do an awesome job.

- ◆ Visualize yourself giving your speech. In your mind, see yourself communicating the appropriate information in a calm and professional manner, speaking clearly, and winning over your prospects.

- ◆ Gain experience. Whether you're making calls or in-person presentations, keep practicing! Experience will help you build up your confidence, reduce your nervousness and speak more effectively. Joining an organization, such as Toastmasters, will help you develop that experience in a nonwork environment where it's okay to learn as you go and make mistakes without the risk of losing clients or turning off prospects.

Speaking with one person on the phone is somewhat easier than communicating with a large group of people. When you're dealing with just one prospect, however, that person needs to be the center of your attention for as long as you're on the telephone. As you develop your rapport with each prospect, try to practice mirroring that person. People like to buy things from people who are just like themselves. Thus, if you see someone is laid back, you should come across as laid back. If someone speaks quickly, try to match his or her speech patterns, in a subtle way, of course. Make a genuine effort to present your information and sales pitch in a manner that will be easily understood by the prospect. This might mean adapting your speech pattern, style, and attitude. If someone has a good sense of humor, work with it. When someone presents himself or herself as being more serious and down to business, you, too, need to adopt that mentality.

Negotiation and Conflict Resolution

When you work with many prospects and clients, it is inevitable that you will encounter some disagreement or a difference in opinion. Developing basic negotiation and conflict-resolution skills will be useful in all of your sales efforts.

The primary purpose of negotiating is to help two individuals or parties reach an agreement that comes close to meeting or perfectly meets each party's needs. These skills can also be used to resolve conflicts. A good negotiation not only works to resolve the disagreement at hand, but also focuses on maintaining a sense of professionalism throughout the negotiation, so they can continue building a strong business relationship with the other party.

The goal of any negotiation is to make both parties happy and create a positive "win-win" situation, as opposed to an "I win, you lose," "you win, I lose," or "I lose, you lose" situation, where one or both parties are not pleased with the outcome.

In a telemarketing situation when trying to make a sale, one of the most common things you may need to negotiate with your prospects about is price. Your goal is to make as much money as possible from the sale and make the biggest sale possible. The potential customer's goal is to spend the least amount of money possible. To reach a satisfactory agreement, you'll most likely need to address many issues, concerns, and questions from the person with whom you're negotiating.

When involved in any negotiation, make sure of the following:

* You know exactly what you want the outcome to be. Although you don't want to share this information, also know the very least that you'd be willing to accept in order to achieve a positive outcome. If you're negotiating on price, go into the negotiation knowing that under no circumstances can you agree to a price of less than a specific number. Although you know the bare minimum of what you'd accept, you want to negotiate for the highest possible price. It's your job to demonstrate why the price of your product/ service is reasonable and how it will ultimately save the customer money or help him or her earn more money, for example.

* You develop a good understanding of what the person you're negotiating with wants the outcome to be and why. What are his or her expectations?

* You're dealing with the proper person who has the authority to make decisions and negotiate on behalf of his or her company or organization.

- You understand each of the issues that need to be discussed and negotiated.
- You're prepared with the information and resources you need to present your arguments. Most often, this will include a thorough understanding of your product/service. When you're totally prepared, you enter into the negotiation in a stronger position, which will make your arguments more effective.
- You're prepared to listen to everything the other person or party has to say. You want to attempt to see and understand things from his or her point of view, whether or not you agree with that position.
- You focus on one issue, problem, or element of the negotiation at a time. Once you reach agreement on one thing, move on to the next. Start with the least complex issues that require the least amount of negotiating.

Negotiations can take on many forms. As a telemarketer, however, you'll typically need to negotiate specific points relating to a sale during telephone conversations. Whether or not you agree with what's being said, a good negotiator never allows his or her emotions to get in their way. Instead, a good negotiator maintains a level head and avoids emotional outbursts or any actions that could be perceived as unprofessional. It's also important to work toward achieving resolutions quickly, especially on smaller issues, while always maintaining a positive attitude. Your primary goal is to help your prospects see things from your perspective and be extremely happy about their decision to work with you and ultimately buy from you. From the prospects' perspective, you want to be someone they believe is helping them achieve their objectives.

Once an agreement is made verbally, make sure both parties are on the same page, so to speak, by reiterating what's been discussed and agreed upon. It's always a good idea to follow up these discussions with a letter (in writing) outlining the issues and the agreed-to outcomes. Remember: Negotiating is about reaching agreement and building upon business relationships. As does any other skill, negotiating will take practice, but you'll quickly see the benefits when you're able to solve disagreements and close sales faster.

Organization

In Chapter 7, all of the steps a telemarketer engages in to ultimately close a sale were outlined. Knowing that you'll be dealing with dozens, perhaps hundreds, of prospects at any given time, it's important to take a highly organized approach to all of your telemarketing efforts. This means keeping detailed records, having all of the information you need at your fingertips, and knowing exactly what actions need to be taken and when.

Lacking organization could easily result in mistakes, missed appointments, missed opportunities, poor customer service, improper follow-through, and other unprofessional behavior that will impact how you and your company are perceived by prospects and clients.

In addition to using contact management software to keep track of all information relating to your prospect/client lists and appointments (see Chapter 13), you need to develop a personal filing system for all paperwork, to insure that these materials are kept organized and are completed in a timely manner. As you'll discover, organizational and time-management skills are closely related.

Keeping your information highly organized will help you prepare as you embark on your telemarketing efforts. With proper preparation comes confidence. This confidence will impact your sales approach and ability to close sales. Because you'll be working with many prospects and/or clients simultaneously, it's an excellent strategy to develop a checklist system, so you can easily track the progress of any individual prospect as you take him or her through your sales cycle.

As you make each call, rate the prospect based on your likelihood to close the sale. Consider developing your own grading system to rate your prospects as you make contact with them. Using an "A" through "D" rating system, for example, here's how you might rate your prospects:

- "A" Prospect = Hot prospect. You can close a sale within 30 days.
- "B" Prospect = Warm prospect. You should be able to close within 60 days.
- "C" Prospect = Viable prospect, but not an immediate lead. In other words, you could probably close a sale within 90 or sometime in the future.
- "D" Prospect = Dead prospect. The prospect should not be considered qualified or viable.

Because your goal is to close sales and generate as much revenue as possible, spend the majority of your time focusing on your "A" prospects. For each prospect/client you begin working with, enter all related information into contact management software and keep detailed notes of all conversations. As you do this, use a worksheet such as the one shown here to help chart your progress with each prospect. You may need to customize the steps on this worksheet to meet your own needs. This is information that could be incorporated into contact management software or recorded on paper as you make your calls.

Prospect Worksheet

Company (Prospect) Name: _____

Contact Person: _____

Contact Person's Title: _____

Phone Number:_____

Fax Number:_____

Mailing Address:_____

_____

E-mail Address:_____

Personal Information (birth date, spouse's name, interests, hobbies, etc.):_____

_____

Name of the Gatekeeper:_____

Steps Taken To Date:

	Date Initiated	Date Completed
Prequalify Prospect		
Initiate Call/Deal With Gatekeeper(s)		
Determine Decision-maker		
Get Decision-maker on the Phone		
Make Sales Pitch		
Send Out Proposal or Letter		
Follow Up		
Close the Sale		
Follow Up With New Customer		

Prospect Rating:_____

To help you chart your progress throughout the day and from week to week, keep a checklist such as the following:

Today's Date:

	Daily Stats
Number of Cold Calls Made	
Number of Decision-makers Reached	
Number of "A" Prospects Contacted	
Number of Proposals Made and Sent Out	
Number of Follow-up Calls Made	
Total Number of Sales Made	

Using technology whenever possible, streamline your paperwork and the busywork associated with telemarketing. Don't try to save time by cutting corners or not doing the necessary paperwork, however.

Stress Management

Every job involves some level of stress. Although telemarketing can be extremely rewarding, making cold calls, meeting sales quotas, and dealing with rejection can certainly elevate your stress level. Many people who suffer from job-related stress do little or nothing to deal with it. Learning how to pinpoint what aspects of your job actually create the frustration and stress you experience, and then discovering ways to eliminate or manage that stress, will help you become a happier person in both your personal and professional life.

If you experience too much stress or frustration at work and have trouble coping, begin by making a detailed list of everything that's wrong with your current employment situation. List all of the things that add to your stress level. Once you've compiled this list, evaluate each item and determine how much control you have over each situation. For example, by changing your basic work habits, schedule, or attitude, could some of your frustration easily be eliminated or reduced?

Once you know the primary things that are making you unhappy, think about the options available to you and find creative ways to reduce your stress level. If, for example, you spend two hours in traffic each day as part of your commute to and from work, simply by altering your work schedule and arriving to work later and then staying later, could you avoid some of the traffic and cut your commute time? Would taking public transportation as opposed to driving your own car help you reduce your commute time? What about car-pooling? Would it be possible for you to work from home and telecommute one or more days per week? By eliminating the amount of time you spend in traffic each day, how much happier would you be in your current job?

Even if the solutions you come up with don't immediately seem feasible, write them down. Next, determine which of your solutions could be acted upon immediately in order to improve your situation. If you have a long-term approach to solving your problems, create a sub-list of easily attainable objectives that will help lead to your ultimate goal or solution. Find ways to simplify your life.

Are you passionate about what you're doing and proud to talk about what you do? One of the biggest reasons people are stressed out on the job is because they're not happy in their job. When people are angry or frustrated, they often act spontaneously, allowing their emotions to dictate their actions. By maintaining better control and spending time thinking about the repercussions of your actions, you'll be in a better position to take control of your professional life. Most importantly, take an active role in finding ways to manage or eliminate the stresses in your professional life. Doing nothing about your situation or simply accepting it will do nothing to improve your situation.

People who overreact to situations often cause much of their own stress. Become an under-reactor. Try taking 10 seconds to 24 hours before responding to any situation you are emotional about. If something has gotten you upset or angry, back off from the situation and evaluate it. Never allow people to push your buttons. There are many people out there who cause aggravation and stress. Just because someone else is negative, don't get caught up in their negative energy.

Find ways to cope with the stress you're experiencing, without allowing it to build up within you. Discovering ways to deal with job-related stresses while still on the job will allow you to go home at the end of each day more relaxed. One of the biggest mistakes people with stressful jobs make is that they take their frustrations home with them and then take out their unhappiness on family and friends.

There may not be an overnight solution for fixing the problem(s) you have at work. However, by taking an aggressive approach to pinpointing the problem areas and finding creative solutions, you will be able to reduce or totally eliminate much of the on-the-job stress and frustration you experience or learn ways of better dealing with it.

Because every person is different, what works for one person may not work for someone else in the same situation. For ideas on how to deal with your situation, ask the people you work with, or other people in your field, how they cope with the job-related stress they experience.

Developing a support system is an excellent strategy for better managing the stress you deal with on a daily basis. Surround yourself with people you enjoy being with. It is okay to

share your thoughts and concerns with others. Surround yourself with positive people at work and take control of your life.

Following are a few strategies for successfully reducing
stress:

- Avoid beverages with caffeine (such as coffee
  or soda), as well as chocolate and excessive
  sugar. Instead, drink herbal tea to help you feel
  more relaxed.

- Close your eyes and take slow, deep breaths to
  quickly calm yourself down.

- Create a more comfortable work environment
  (use a more comfortable chair, add better light-
  ing, and/or better personalize your workspace).

- Develop a support group, consisting of coworkers, friends, family members or others who are
  experiencing a similar situation or who understand
  what you're going through.

- If one person is causing you frustration, approach
  that person on a friendly level to discuss the situation, without causing a confrontation. Try to work
  out mutually beneficial solutions together.

- If you feel depressed on an ongoing basis, consult your doctor.

- Listen to soothing music.

- Make an appointment for a massage.

- When experiencing an overly stressful situation,
  take a short break. Go for a walk outside of your
  work area and clear your head.

- Work out or exercise several times per week.

Time Management

Are you always running late for appointments? Do the items
on your daily to-do list never seem to get done fast enough? If

there is never enough time in your day to meet your personal and professional obligations, you could be lacking important time-management skills.

Learning time-management skills won't add more hours to the workday, but it will allow you to use all of your time more productively, reduce the stress in your life, better focus on what's important, and ultimately get more done faster.

Time management is easy to learn and requires just one basic tool: a daily planner, personal digital assistant, or specialized scheduling software for your computer. Daily planners or schedulers are available from office supply stores or directly from companies, such as Day Timers ((800) 854–0346/ *www.daytimer.com*). They come in a variety of sizes, designed to fit on a desk or within a jacket pocket or purse, plus they're available in many different daily, weekly, and monthly formats.

A personal digital assistant (PDA) is a handheld electronic device that can be used to store hundreds of contact names and addresses, appointments, notes, and other pieces of information. PDAs range in price based on their capabilities. PDAs, such as the Palm (*www.palm.com*), for example, can be used to manage scheduling, organize to-do lists, and track other important information. Many software programs for desktop computers, such as Microsoft Outlook or ACT!, can also be used to manage scheduling and help users better manage their time.

It's important to choose a time-management tool that you're comfortable with, whether it's a traditional planner, a high-tech device, or a specialized software package. The tool you choose for yourself should easily fit your work habits and professional lifestyle. If you're always on the go, you'll want a planner or PDA that's totally portable and can be carried with you. If most of your time is spent working from a desk and talking on the telephone, a desktop planner or software package for your desktop computer may be best suited to meet your needs.

Once you obtain a time-management tool, spend several days carefully analyzing how you spend every minute of your day. Determine what takes up the majority of your time, but diminishes your productivity. Perhaps you experience countless interruptions from coworkers, you don't have well-defined priorities, your work area is messy and disorganized, you have too much to do and become overwhelmed, or you're constantly forced to participate in unscheduled meetings.

As you examine how you spend your day, pinpoint the biggest time-wasters that are keeping you from getting your most important work done. According to the Day Timer's 4-Dimensional Time Management program, an audio cassette–, video-, or CD-ROM-based course that teaches time-management skills, to successfully manage your time you must learn how to:

- ◆ Focus. Determine what's really important and what duties you need to perform in a timely manner. Learn to differentiate between what's important and what's not in terms of how you spend your time.

- ◆ Plan. Discover how to properly prioritize your work and the items on your to-do list. Set goals based on your work objectives and figure out, in advance, how much time each task will take.

- ◆ Act. Based on your planning, take an organized approach to completing each of the high-priority tasks and items on your to-do list. Focus on the less important items and tasks later.

Every evening (after work) or first thing in the morning, take about 15 minutes to create a daily to-do list. After listing all of the things that need to get done that day, determine approximately how long each task will take. Now, set your priorities. On your to-do list, place an "A" next to the items or tasks that will produce the most valuable results. These are the items that must get done, no matter what.

Next, go back to the top of your list and place a "B" next to important tasks that need to get done, but that aren't as critical or time-sensitive as your "A" items. Finally, place a "C" next to items or tasks that should get done, but that aren't too important. During a day or week, the priority level of a task may change.

Take major projects, goals, and objectives and divide them into smaller, more manageable tasks. You'll need to incorporate your to-do list into your daily planner, allowing you to schedule your time. Make sure you attempt to complete your high-priority items and tasks early in the day, giving those items your full attention.

Once you commit to using a time-management tool, it's important to remain disciplined enough and use it continuously until it becomes second nature. Initially, you may have to spend up to 30 minutes per day planning your time and creating your to-do list, but ultimately you'll begin saving up to several hours per day. Learning to better manage your time will boost your productivity. (Additional information about PDAs and scheduling software can be found in Chapter 13.)

Obtaining and Enhancing Your Personal Skill Set

No matter how good your skills already are, it's important to constantly work toward improving your professional skill set and to continue honing your telemarketing skills. There are many ways to obtain the skills described in this chapter as well as other skills you'll find helpful as you pursue your career. Although enrolling in school to obtain additional education will definitely be beneficial, this solution for obtaining skills isn't always practical for people working full-time. Instead of attending a traditional college or graduate school (during the day or evenings), other options for improving your education and building your skill set include:

- Reading "how-to" books.
- Attending professional seminars and trade shows.
- Listening to instructional audiotapes. If you have to commute to work, utilizing your time traveling by listening to audio courses is an excellent investment of your time. You'll find a wide range of audio courses and motivational programs available on cassette and compact disc. Verbal Advantage (described in Chapter 6) is just one example.
- Learning from your coworkers. Get formal hands-on training and critique from your coworkers and/or superiors, or study their success and try to incorporate their successful strategies into your activities. Single out the most talented salespeople within your organization and watch them at work. Study their technique and learn from their experience. If another salesperson at your company is doing better than you, that's great news! It demonstrates to you there is potential for you to do better. Try to make more calls or perfect your pitch to land more sales. Try to beat your previous record for the number of calls made per day as well as the number of sales made per day.
- Subscribing to professional or industry-oriented newsletters and magazines.
- Doing research on the Internet to learn about specific topics and learn new skills.
- Participating in mock sales presentations and role-playing with your coworkers in order to perfect your specific sales presentation and hone your skills. When practicing with others, make a point to rehearse your sales pitch, practice handling objections, and work on new and innovative ways

for closing sales. Be creative in setting up realistic scenarios, then engage in role-play exercises to play out those scenarios.

◆ Soliciting and accepting feedback from your clients. Once you have developed a strong rapport with your clients, send out a survey or questionnaire to learn what you could be doing better. This will allow you to learn how prospects and clients feel about you, your company, and your product/service. Determine what needs your customers have that you could be filling and adapt that knowledge when dealing with current and future prospects and clients.

In terms of your overall telephone skills, throughout this book you've been reading strategies for acquiring and improving upon your ability to use the telephone as your primary tool for generating sales. Of course, you can measure your skills based upon how quickly and easily you're able to close sales, however, you can always fine-tune your telesales skills by evaluating your performance on an ongoing basis, plus having others (your supervisor or coworkers) offer you valuable and honest feedback.

This can be done by recording your sales calls and then later reviewing your performance to analyze what you could have done better. It's always important to learn from your mistakes, identify what you're doing right, and discover new ways of improving your sales skills. By carefully evaluating your strengths and weaknesses, you can learn how to utilize your strengths while downplaying or overcoming your weaknesses. Once you've made several sales calls, answer the following questions to help you evaluate and improve your performance.

What are some of your best strengths as a telemarketer?

_____

_____

_____

What are your biggest weaknesses?

_____

_____

_____

How can you begin to improve upon those weaknesses and eventually overcome them? What specific game plan can you adopt for accomplishing this, starting immediately?

_____

_____

_____

Based on your telemarketing and sales experience thus far, what are the primary reasons why you personally are not closing the number of sales you want? What's holding you back?

_____

_____

_____

◆ ◆ ◆

As you answer the previous questions, ask yourself: Are you properly identifying and qualifying prospects? Are you making enough calls? Are you having trouble getting through to the appropriate decision-maker(s)? Are you getting your message across effectively? Do you forget to ask closing questions or recognize the "buying" signals given off by your prospects? Do you forget to ask for the sale after making your pitch? Are you following up properly with your prospects? Once you've made a sale, are you working hard enough to offer top-notch customer service and provide the support needed by your customers? Do your prospects and clients respect you? You need to answer these questions honesty, then pick areas you feel you can improve on and work on those specific things.

Your professional skill set is your personal toolbox for success. After you've developed each of your skills, work on an ongoing basis to perfect them, plus find new and innovative ways to incorporate those skills into your work-related efforts. Combine your skills with your knowledge and experience to become an expert in your field. Being a successful telesales professional isn't easy, but, by utilizing your skills in conjunction with the other strategies described within this book you'll be well on your way to having the knowledge and abilities needed to achieve your goals. (You'll find additional strategies for perfecting your telemarketing skills in Chapter 11 and Chapter 14.)

Chapter 10

TELEMARKETING
SCRIPTS

From the moment you say "hello" and introduce yourself when making a cold call or responding to an incoming call from a prospect or customer, the wording you use is one of the major components of a successful telemarketing campaign. No matter what you're selling, developing a well-written script or sales pitch will help you achieve greater success when telemarketing. As you already know from Chapter 6, however, simply reading a script won't help you make sales. As a telemarketing or telesales professional, you need to present that script in a way that's exciting and interesting for the prospect to hear. Ideally, you also want the sales pitch to be interactive, meaning there's two-way dialogue between you and your prospect.

Writing a sales script that works is very different from writing a business letter, for example. The wording you use and the overall writing style of a telemarketing script needs to be upbeat and take on a conversational style and tone. The person reading the script should not sound as though he or she is reading. After all, it's pretty obvious to tell when a telemarketer is reading a poorly written script word for word and when he or she is using a well-written script to present their sales pitch.

This chapter is all about developing a telemarketing script that will achieve the results you want. Although every script will be different, based on the product/service you're selling, every telemarketing script has a few key components and a specific style. In this chapter, you'll learn several important strategies for writing an effective telemarketing script, learn who to contact if you need assistance developing your script, and also be able to read and analyze some actual telemarketing scripts that have been used successfully by telemarketers and call centers. These sample scripts have been annotated with information to help you understand important points and strategies that have been embedded into these scripts.

Who Should Write Your Telemarketing Script?

The telemarketing script you develop for yourself or your company should have several objectives. It should:

- Introduce you *and* your company to the prospect.
- State the reason for your call.
- Describe, in detail, your product/service.
- Explain the benefits and features of your product/service.
- Demonstrate how your product/service can solve a problem your prospect has.
- Be well-written, easy to understand, and informative.
- Address objections you know a prospect might have—before the prospect has a chance to bring them up.

- ◆ Constantly be focusing on or working toward closing a sale or achieving a predetermined goal (such as setting an appointment or gathering information).

To accomplish all of these tasks, you should receive input about the content of your script from people who are knowledgeable about what you're offering. This input can come from people who are experts in marketing, from people associated with your company who communicate well in writing, and from the people who will actually be doing the telemarketing. Remember that it's the telemarketers who will be the people actually presenting the script and interacting with the prospects. An effective telemarketing script is not something you'll be able to create quickly off the top of your head. It's something that should evolve through a series of revisions and trials, as you pinpoint what key sales messages you need to communicate (see Chapter 4) and what the best method to convey that information is. Ideally, you'll want a team of people with various areas of expertise to contribute to your telemarketing script to insure it achieves all of its objectives. Then, you want to test that script to insure it has the impact you desire on the intended audience.

Remember that a written sales letter, product brochure, or press release is very different from a telemarketing script. Although the concepts you're trying to convey may be the same, how you word these various documents will differ greatly. As an experiment, try reading out loud any business correspondence you've received recently, or try reading the text from a catalog. If you were hearing this read over the telephone, would it sound like a natural conversation? Would it sound interesting and hold your attention? Would it be easily understandable? The answer to these questions is probably not, mainly because these documents were meant to be read, not heard.

Writing a powerful telemarketing script is an art form, almost akin to writing fiction or poetry. It takes knowledge, skill, and practice. If you've never written this type of document before, and you're anxious to kick off you're telemarketing efforts, you might consider hiring a professional telemarketing script writer to either write your script from scratch or fine-tune what you've already created.

Later in this chapter, you'll read an interview with Robert Kaufman, the president of ScriptingPower ((203) 229–0025/ *www.scriptingpower.com*), a Connecticut-based company. ScriptingPower specializes in writing telemarketing scripts for well-known companies that are looking to stop hang-ups, keep potential customers on the telephone, increase sales, and encourage prospects to ask questions and keep the conversation interactive. As you'll learn, investing the money necessary to hire a professional scriptwriter can dramatically improve the success of your overall telemarketing efforts.

Whether you're doing inbound or outbound telemarketing, the script you use is important. In addition to ScriptingPower, there are dozens, perhaps hundreds, of other professional scriptwriters and organizations available on a short-term consulting basis to help you achieve success. If you'll be hiring an outside call center to handle your company's telemarketing needs, chances are that call center will work directly with you to develop your script. Many advertising agencies also specialize in creating this type of material.

Several other specialized telemarketing script-writing companies include:

- 5-Star Telemarketing ((732) 842–8126/ *www.5star-telemarketing.com*).
- Advisory Group ((916) 974–3511/ *advisorygroupmkt.com/html*).
- InCredible English ((800) 994–8409/ *www.incredibleenglish.com*).

- Phonedamentals ((888) 738–8388/ *phonedamentals.com*).
- Sarno Services ((757) 427–0738/ *www.sarnoservices.com*).

The Elements of an Outbound Telemarketing Script

Although every telemarketing script will be different, each will have key elements in common. The key elements you'll find in an outbound telemarketing script include the following:

- Introduction. Identify yourself and your company. Say something along the lines of, "Hi, this is John Smith, I am calling on behalf of the XYZ Company to tell you about...."
- Interest-creating comment (a.k.a. "The Hook"). In less than 15 seconds (one or two sentences), you need to capture your prospect's attention. This is probably the most important line of the script, because it plays a major role in determining if a prospect will stay on the phone with you or hang up. For example, state, "I'm calling to tell you about how companies such as yours have successfully saved up to $200 per month simply by using our new [insert product name]. Would you enjoy experiencing this level of savings, starting almost immediately?" (Pause and wait for a response.)
- Build rapport. During this phase of the call, you need to befriend the prospect. You might ask, "Do you have a minute?"
- Qualify the prospect. Make sure you're talking to the decision-maker and that there's a need or desire for your product/service. For example, if

you're selling advertising, you might ask, "Who is the person who purchases the advertising for your company?"

* Ask questions. Use open-ended questions to gain valuable insight into your customer's needs, wants, and problems. A good telemarketer will allow the prospect to do most of the talking.

* Main sales pitch. Explain what you're offering, its benefits, its features, and your main sales points. Focus on problem solving features as you address the needs of your prospect.

* Trial close. Try to close the sale. There are many closing methods you can incorporate. (See Chapter 8 for details.) You'll ultimately want to have prepared at least three closing strategies you can use during each call.

* Handling objections and concerns. Ask questions, pinpoint objections, soften the objections, and address them one at a time. This is done by confirming an understanding of the objection, showing empathy by making a statement such as, "I understand what you're saying," stressing benefits and then addressing each objection head on.

* Trial close. After dealing with the first round of objections, try to close the sale again.

* Handling additional objections and concerns. At this stage, you may need to incorporate basic negotiation strategies to achieve your objectives and overcome objections, such as price.

* The close. This should be the point in the conversation when you achieve the call's objective, such as making a sale or setting an appointment for an in-person sales call.

- ◆ Concluding the call. Thank the customer for his or her order and/or achieve some level of agreement in terms of what was discussed. Talk about what will happen next, such as a follow-up call, you sending information, the preparation of a sales contract, and so on, and then say goodbye.

Telemarketing Script-Writing Strategies

First and foremost, it's important to develop an understanding of who will be using the script and how closely the script will be followed. For example, if you have dozens or hundreds of telemarketers working from a call center on a telemarketing campaign, you'll want those people to stick with your script and present it word for word. This means you need to create a "verbatim" typescript.

When highly skilled and experienced telemarketers are selling higher-end products or services, and these people have a thorough knowledge and understanding of your product/service, they will often use a telemarketing script as a general guideline but will ultimately use some of their own selling and improvisational skills to close each sale. In this situation, a "guided" script is more appropriate.

As soon as you've created what you believe to be the perfect telemarketing script for whatever it is you're selling, start testing that script. See how effective the script is in terms of achieving your objectives. Start off by having coworkers or friends act as prospects as you rehearse the script. Next, call on some sample prospects and try your script. You want to test the script at least 20 times before finally implementing it into your telemarketing efforts.

If you're creating your own telemarketing script in-house, as you write, be clear, concise, conversational, and convincing. Following are a few guidelines and strategies you might incorporate into your efforts:

- Define the goal of your telemarketing script. Are you trying to sell a product/service, obtain an appointment, gather information from the prospect, sell to repeat customers, up-sell additional products/services, or achieve some other goal?

- Encourage dialogue with the prospect. Ask questions and build possible responses into the script. Never ask more than one or two questions in a row. You're not interrogating your prospects. Instead, you're trying to learn from them while at the same time selling to them.

- Use short sentences with relatively simple wording. The telemarketer has to read your script as if he or she is holding a conversation. Thus, use only words that you'd typically hear in a normal conversation.

- Make sure you address the target customers with your script. Think about their needs, their desires, and the solutions that will help them.

- Write the script to be read aloud. You want to make sure the wording is easy to say and that you incorporate the appropriate pauses.

- Give the script an upbeat and motivational tone. Use descriptive words and phrases that will get the prospect excited by creating positive images in their minds. Make sure what the script says, however, is believable. Avoid outlandish comments. In terms of using upbeat wording, you could say, "I have a proposal I'd like to talk with you about." A better way of saying this might be, "I have an exciting opportunity you'll want to take a look at!"

- Incorporate the prospect's name several times into the script.

- ◆ Be brief and to the point. If you can explain something well in one sentence, don't use a paragraph. The people you'll be selling to are busy. You want to make your pitch, deal with objections, and close a sale.
- ◆ Don't use words or phrases that can be misinterpreted because they have multiple meanings.

Meet a Telemarketing Scriptwriting Expert

Even if you're a highly skilled salesperson with a proven track record or if you're the owner of a company and you know everything there is to know about your product/service, that doesn't necessarily mean you'll be able to write a highly effective telemarketing script. A really good script combines a strong knowledge of a product/service with expert marketing strategies and top-notch writing skills. It involves knowing who the customer is and what his or her buying habits are and being able to write a script that motivates that target customer to make a purchase over the telephone.

Telemarketing scriptwriting is a skill and art form that takes a lot of practice. It's also a science, because it involves truly understanding how and why people choose to make purchases over the telephone. Writing a script that will be used for telemarketing is a lot more involved than simply writing a speech, and it's different from creating other types of marketing materials, such as catalogs, brochures, or advertisements.

Robert Kaufman is the president of ScriptingPower ((203) 229–0025/*www.scriptingpower.com*), a company that specializes in helping companies of all sizes write highly effective telemarketing scripts for a wide range of applications. Over the years, the company has written hundreds of inbound and outbound telemarketing scripts for companies including America Online, Fleet Bank, Pizza Hut, Sears, Sara Lee, Pitney Bowes, The Home Shopping Network, and countless smaller companies.

"We are expert telemarketing script writers," explains Kaufman. "When any size companies need a telemarketing script, we use specialized tools and techniques that will allow us to help them maximize their results in terms of sales per hour, conversation rates and call times, for example. We write the main body of the script, but equally important, we create scripted rebuttals for all of the objections prospects may come up with."

When a new client approaches ScriptingPower looking for help developing and testing a telemarketing script, Kaufman and his staff begin by working with the client to learn as much as possible about the product/service that will be sold, what the objectives of the calls will be, and who the target audience is. Using this information, in conjunction with the client's sales brochures, product literature, and other data, ScriptingPower's writers then develop a draft of a script. This script is then given to the client for feedback and is tested before it is fully implemented.

"Our clients need to understand that a tremendous amount of time and effort goes into writing a custom written script for a client. There are a lot of different tricks and tools, as well as proven techniques and marketing strategies that need to be successfully woven into a script. Writing a telemarketing script involves a lot more than throwing words down on paper," adds Kaufman. "Writing a good script is a process. We might go back and forth with the client two times or 10 times while the script is being drafted until we develop something that will be successful. After the script is completed, once it gets tested, it's then tweaked. The whole process can take anywhere from one to four weeks."

According to Kaufman, companies that have never ex-perimented with telemarketing and don't fully understand how to use this sales tool will often make mistakes when developing their own telemarketing scripts. "We found that companies may know all about their product or service, but they don't truly know how to market it. They think they can get on the phone, talk to people and everyone will automatically be interested in making a purchase and giving their credit card information to a stranger who calls them on the phone. In reality, the product or service needs to be properly positioned and the script needs to be developed in such a way that people will stay on the phone long enough to learn about what's being sold," says Kaufman. "One common mistake is that companies that aren't well-known by the consumer think they can make a call cold call to a prospect to obtain a credit card order over the telephone within a few minutes. These days, people are extremely unwilling to give personal information to strangers over the telephone, especially if they've never heard of the company that's calling them."

The goal of a telemarketing script is to convey messages over the telephone. Kaufman explains, "When someone receives a sales letter or product literature, they can read it over and over and focus in on certain portions of the material. With telemarketing, however, you have one chance to make an impression and you have to work quickly. People aren't listening to every single word that's said. They're listening to phrases. A telemarketing script needs to use verbiage that's as short and concise as possible, yet the message needs to be communicated clearly and in a manner that's easily understood by the prospect. The goal is not just for the prospect to hear the message that's being communicated, but in their mind they need to process that message and come to the conclusion that they need what you're selling. Often, success depends on the telemarketer's ability to create tangible ideas in the prospect's mind. They need to be able to clearly imagine the product or service you're selling, [because] they can't see or feel it over the telephone."

How you go about writing the script and what's actually said in the script will vary greatly, based on what's being sold, who the target customer is[,] and how well the prospect already knows the company that's doing the telemarketing. "[Although] every script is different, and there are many different goals a telemarketer might try to accomplish using their script, each script will have some key elements. There's the opening, the introduction to the person you're speaking with, the presentation, the qualified trial close and the actual close," says Kaufman. "Your script needs to cater to the demographics it is targeted to. Every concept that's conveyed and every message you communicate needs to appeal to that target customer. It's all about strategically positioning your product or service, and that positioning will vary greatly based on what's being sold and to whom you're selling to."

No matter what you're selling, Kaufman believes that the single most important element of any telemarketing script is its hook. "Not having a strong enough hook at the beginning of the script and not allowing the prospect to talk at all during the pitch are two common mistakes novice script writers make. Remember, you're not writing a speech. People on the other end of the phone who you are calling won't listen to speeches," says Kaufman.

In addition to all of the sales and marketing strategies that need to be worked into a telemarketing script for it to be successful, Kaufman added that the script also needs to pay careful attention to legal matters. "There are a lot of legalities in terms of what can and can't be said and when things need to be said during a telephone call, and these laws are constantly changing. These legal matters need to be taken into consideration," adds Kaufman, who recommends running a script past a lawyer who specializes in telemarketing laws.

For a company that's developing a new telemarketing script, Kaufman suggests comparing it to an old script in terms of its success rate as the new script is being tested. "Testing a script is critical. If the script isn't working, you need to determine exactly why. By monitoring calls, you can determine when and why prospects are saying 'no' and tweak that script. At this point, feedback from the telemarketers actually making the calls is extremely helpful. I like to invest at least 20 hours worth of calling into the testing phase in order to get a clear idea of how prospects react to it," he adds.

When tweaking a script, Kaufman explains that it's important to make only one or two changes at a time, then go back and test. If you make too many changes at once, it's impossible to determine which changes worked and which ones didn't. "You need to determine the impact of each change you make to a script and not deal with too many variables at one. It might take a full day or two to test each change," says Kaufman.

Based on what you, the telemarketer, or your company is trying to accomplish, you may or may not wish to hire the services of a professional telemarketing scriptwriter to either create a script or help you polish your existing script. Some companies choose to invest in hiring a professional scriptwriter right at the start to insure maximum results. Other companies create their own script, experiment with it, and only seek out professional guidance if what they create doesn't ultimately achieve the desired results.

"Obviously, I'm going to say that everyone should take advantage of the services a company like ScriptingPower offers, because we know things from experience. We've created and tested thousands of scripts. We know what works, what doesn't and what most likely will work for each of our clients. We use strategies that most telemarketers wouldn't think of when creating their own script," states Kaufman. "Our advice and recommendations are based on our writing experience, and on our marketing and sales knowledge. We can help our clients better position their product or service, not just create the words to sell it over the telephone."

Hiring a professional telemarketing scriptwriter involves the same process as hiring any other type of consultant. You'll want to determine that the person or company you're hiring has more experience than you do, has a proven track record, can provide case studies or utilize specialized techniques that will help you achieve your goals, is someone you can work with easily over a period of time. "Look at the writer's past performance and test their knowledge when you're initially speaking with the script writer," says Kaufman, who stated that the cost of hiring a telemarketing scriptwriter can vary greatly. "The costs totally depend on the project. Be prepared to invest anywhere from $750 to $2,500 for a script, plus additional costs for related consulting services."

Is hiring a professional scriptwriter a prerequisite for telemarketing success? Certainly not! However, by investing the time and money necessary to create the most powerful script possible, you'll save later when your telemarketing efforts begin. A well-written script will lead to more closed sales, fewer hang-ups and rejections, less frustration and wasted time, higher revenues, and greater overall success.

Chapter 11

SALES TECHNIQUES
THE PROS USE

By now, you probably realize that being a successful telemarketer involves a lot more than simply picking up the telephone and having a friendly chat with a perspective customer or client. In addition to research and preparation, it's important to pay careful attention to the small details involved in the telemarketing process.

The strategies described within this chapter have been collected from some of the country's leading telemarketing and sales experts. Each has been proven to work effectively in virtually any telephone-based sales situation, so use this information to give yourself the edge you need as a telemarketing professional.

You'll soon be making many telemarketing calls. Although only a percentage of those calls will actually lead to a sale, it's important that you approach each and every call with the same high level of enthusiasm, dedication, sincerity, and attentiveness.

Strategy #1

Dress Like a Pro and Act Like One, Too

Although you may never actually meet your prospects in person, many telemarketing experts agree that it's important to dress professionally when making telephone sales calls. No matter where you're making your sales calls from, dress as if you'll be engaged in a face-to-face business meeting with your prospect. If you're dressed professionally, you're more apt to act professionally over the phone. This will help you get into and stay in the proper state of mind as you are making calls. The tone of your voice, your attitude and confidence level, as well as how you convey yourself over the phone, correlate directly to how you're dressed and how you perceive yourself.

Some telemarketers who work from home not only dress as if they're about to engage in an in-person business meeting, at the start of their day, they also leave their home and take a short drive before beginning their workday. During this short drive, the telemarketers will spend their time getting into the right frame of mind for the workday ahead. They might also plan their day and think about (or rehearse) their sales pitch before returning home to begin making their calls.

If you're working from a home office, remember to keep all ancillary noises to an absolute minimum. The people you're calling should never hear your dog barking or baby crying, for example. If space allows, create a totally separate work environment for yourself that's removed from your normal living space. No matter where you're telemarketing from, the people you're calling should hear only you, not other telemarketers in the room (or call center). The objective is to quickly develop a clear line of communication between you and the prospect and anything that gets in the way of that objective should be eliminated.

Strategy #2

Set Daily, Weekly, and Monthly Goals for Yourself

Before launching your telemarketing effort, spend time developing a series of realistic goals for yourself. Establishing goals will keep you motivated and on track. For example, for each month, determine how many sales you need to make (and/or how many new clients you need to bring in) in order to reach your financial objectives. Based on this information, you can create daily and weekly goals.

Determine your sales cycles as quickly as possible. This means learning how long it takes (and what's required) for you to make a single sale. For example, if you're looking to generate $50,000 in sales per month, and your average sale amount is $10,000, to reach your goal, you need to make five sales per month. Along the way, if you determine that it takes 50 calls in order to make a single sale, then you realistically need to make 500 calls per month in order to generate your desired income, so plan accordingly.

For each day, part of your planning should include determining:

- The number of total calls that need to be made.
- The number of new prospects you need to reach.
- The number of follow-up calls that need to be made to new prospects.
- The number of calls to current clients that need to be made.

Strategy #3

Manage Your Time Effectively

Make an appointment with yourself to call upon new customers. This means set aside a specific amount of time per day to do this, based on your goals. Be sure to call your prospects when they're most likely to be in and willing to take your call. If calling a restaurant owner, for example, don't call during peak meal hours. Instead, call when you know the decision-maker is most likely to be accessible and will be available to speak with you. Use a daily planner or scheduling software to pre-plan your days.

Strategy #4

Prequalify Your Prospects

Telemarketing is a labor-intensive and time-consuming process. To make this easier and reduce the number of calls you'll need to make before actually making each sale, do the necessary research and prequalify your prospects before ever picking up the telephone. Once you know the person or company you're calling has a definite need or desire for your product/service, determine the appropriate person to speak with in order to make your sale. Sometimes, determining who the decision-maker is within an organization and reaching that person can be one of the biggest challenges you'll face. Keep in mind that there may be multiple decision-makers you'll need to deal with in order to close a single sale.

Once you've created a call list of prospects, sort through the list and give priority to those people or companies you identify as being the most likely to want or need your product/service. You also want to identify those prospects that can easily afford what you're offering, and you want to understand each prospect's business cycle. For example, your client may only have the necessary funding or need for your product/service during specific times of the year.

Strategy #5

Watch Yourself Work

Because there's no in-person contact between you and your prospects, it's vital that you convey the necessary amount of energy and enthusiasm over the telephone. Even though a prospect can't actually see you smiling, your smile will be apparent in the tone of your voice, so make sure it's present during each call.

Many expert telemarketers actually place a mirror in front of them when making calls. As they look at themselves in the mirror, they picture the prospect they're talking to. This allows you, the telemarketer, to see how the prospect would see you. Are you smiling? Are you lively enough? Do you look sincere? When looking in the mirror during a telemarketing call, ask yourself, "Would I buy from myself?"

It's also an excellent strategy to record some or all of your calls so you can later go back and evaluate your performance to determine what needs to be improved.

Strategy #6

Develop Your Script

As you get to know the product/service you're selling, it's an excellent idea to develop a detailed script and to keep that script in front of you while you're making calls. Your script should include:

- An introduction.
- A description of what you do and/or have to offer.
- A list of answers to common objections (and strategies for handling them).

- ◆ Answers to common questions prospects might have.
- ◆ Several closing strategies.

Without making it obvious, feel free to refer to your script during the sales call. However, when you're not making calls, spend as much time as is necessary to rehearse your script and practice your sales pitch. You never want to sound as though you're reading a script or simply reciting a canned speech you've memorized word for word. With practice, you want to develop a presentation that makes you sound natural, lively, knowledgeable, credible, and enthusiastic.

Strategy #7

Reward Yourself

Life as a telemarketer involves making countless calls throughout each and every day. To break up the monotony and to keep yourself motivated, reward yourself for achieving pre-defined goals. The reward you set for yourself should be proportionate to your success. For example, for every 50 calls you make, reward yourself with a five-minute break. For each sale you make, reward yourself with a nice dinner at your favorite restaurant. Other potential mini-rewards throughout your day might include making a personal call, taking a walk, or having a snack or a cup of coffee.

If one of your personal long-term goals is to buy a luxury car, buy a boat, send your children to college, or purchase a new home, keep a picture of what you're striving for on your desk and refer to it often. Remember that with each sale you make, you're one step closer to purchasing that dream car, boat, college education, or home.

Strategy #8

Handle Rejection Effectively

Rejection is part of the telemarketing process. Unfortunately, no matter how good of a salesperson you are, not every prospect you call will have a want or need for what you're offering. Remember, however, that for every "no" or hang-up you experience, you're one step closer to that all-important "yes."

If you know it takes 50 calls to make a single sale, even if you have received 20 rejections in a row, you only have an average of 30 more calls to make before closing your next sale. No matter what the person on the other end of the telephone says to you during a call, never take rejection personally!

Even if someone says no right now, he or she could become a viable prospect in the future, so don't burn any bridges. Try to determine his or her future needs and decide if he or she is a worthwhile prospect to contact in the future. In some cases, you may determine the person or company you just called isn't ever going to be a viable prospect. In this case, cross that prospect off your list and move on to the next one.

Strategy #9

Always Listen to Your Prospects and Customers

Once you get the appropriate decision-maker on the telephone and begin making your pitch, incorporate as many open-ended questions as possible. Get the prospect to speak openly. Develop a two-way dialogue. When the prospect is speaking, listen carefully to what's being said and take notes. Listening is the most valuable tool for learning about your prospect. Never underestimate it.

As you begin to learn about your prospect, customize your sales pitch based on his or her needs, wants, thoughts, and opinions. If you're speaking and you get interrupted, allow the potential customer to speak and listen carefully to what he or she has to say.

Strategy #10

Close the Deal

This may sound obvious and like common sense, however, one of the biggest reasons why telemarketers fail to make their sale is because they never actually ask for the deal. At some point during your call, you need to ask for the sale. As important as it is to address the prospect's needs and provide a solution, at the appropriate time, you also need to come right out and ask him or her to buy what you're offering. You may need to do this a few times in the later stages of your pitch to generate the desired result.

Strategy #11

Foster Your Current Relationships

Transforming a new prospect into a valuable customer is often a difficult process. Thus, once you've landed new customers, don't neglect them. It's important for telemarketers to foster and build upon their existing relationships in order to generate new business, either directly with that customer or through referrals. You'll quickly discover that earning repeat business from a satisfied customer is a lot easier than generating a sale from a new prospect.

Each time you call an existing client, work toward developing a friendly rapport. This will help insure that your future calls will be taken by the customer. As you're fostering your relationships with existing clients, don't push hard for a sale every time you make contact. Instead, periodically call the client to see how things are going in terms of how they're doing with your product/service, as well as in general. As you learn personal information about your client (children's names, hobbies, birthdays, anniversaries, and so forth), be sure to refer back to this information during subsequent calls to develop a more personalized relationship.

As the salesperson, try to offer your clients information that might help their business. For example, if you see a newspaper or magazine article that would be of interest to a customer/client, cut it out and send it to him or her with a personal note.

Strategy #12

Work Without Interruptions

It's important to set aside specific times to make your telemarketing calls. When engaged in this activity, don't distract yourself with other tasks or by answering incoming calls. If necessary, to avoid unwanted interruptions, shut the door to your office and concentrate on the task at hand; all you should be doing is making outbound calls when you're engaged in a telemarketing effort. Interruptions could easily cause you to lose focus and break your rhythm.

Strategy #13

Keep Yourself Organized and Take Good Notes

Once you start making dozens of calls in a single day, keeping track of who you called, what was discussed, who you actually made contact with, and who needs a follow-up call, for example, will get extremely confusing if you don't take an organized approach to your telemarketing efforts.

In addition to keeping a copy of your telemarketing script in front of you, maintain a detailed call list and keep it handy. During or after each call, write down detailed notes about what happened during the call and what needs to be done next. When you actually get the right person on the phone and begin to make your pitch, refer to your notes from past discussions.

Some of the information you'll want to include in your notes are:

+ When you called.
+ With whom you spoke.
+ What was discussed.
+ What follow up needs to be taken and when.
+ Details about who else within the company you need to speak with.
+ Information about the customer's needs, wants, and budget.
+ Personal information about the decision-maker.

Strategy #14

Deal Effectively With Screeners and Gatekeepers

Many decision-makers have secretaries or receptionists who determine which incoming calls get through and which don't. Always be polite and act professionally when dealing with gatekeepers. These people have the power to help you get in touch with the person you need to speak with, so make an effort to win them over and solicit their help. Get to know these people by name. They can easily provide you with valuable information about your prospect, such as the best time to call or the best approach to take in trying to reach him or her.

Most business leaders take the opinions of their support staff seriously. If a gatekeeper, for example, mentions to the decision-maker that you were rude, that could jeopardize your ability to close a sale.

When you're dealing with a gatekeeper, identify yourself by name. Briefly state your business and find out who the best person to speak with is within the organization. Ask for the gatekeeper's help, but keep in mind that he or she may be juggling multiple tasks at once and may not have the time to chit-chat with you.

Strategy #15

Use Voice Mail to Your Advantage

There will be many times that you'll be forwarded to someone's voice mail. Instead of looking at this as a brush-off, leave a message and use this opportunity to your advantage. Identify yourself and let the prospect know what you do and why you're calling. Briefly tell the prospect you may have a way to help him or her with his or her business and that you'd like a chance to speak on the phone to see if there's a good match. In your message, try to create urgency, giving the decision-maker a reason he or she should call you back quickly. When leaving your message, keep it short. Your goal is simply to entice the decision-maker to return your call.

Strategy #16

Make the Internet Work for You

Use the Internet to your advantage. The Web can be used to find and research prospects and/or information about clients. You can get news about almost any company either by visiting its Website directly or using a search engine (such as

Yahoo.com or Google.com) and entering the company's name as a search phrase.

Incorporating These Strategies

Review these strategies often, until implementing them automatically becomes part of your ongoing telemarketing routine. In the next chapter, you'll discover some of the most common mistakes telemarketers make so you can easily avoid them.

Chapter 12

COMMON TELEMARKETING MISTAKES TO AVOID

A s the telemarketing professional, the positive relation-ship you're able to build with your prospect, starting from the moment a phone call is made, is critical. Your overall objective is always to close a sale, but to reach that point, your ongoing goal should be to foster that positive rela-tionship and build trust with each prospect.

Thus far, *Top Telemarketing Techniques* has focused on the steps needed to transform you into a top-notch telemarketer as you implement your own successful telemarketing campaign. You've probably discovered by now that there are no easy shortcuts for closing a sale. Ongoing attention to detail will rep-resent the difference between a hang-up, a "sorry, we're not interested," and a sale.

Even if you do your research and preparation, then follow each of the steps outlined in this book, there are a few potential pitfalls you'll want to avoid. This chapter focuses on the most common mistakes made by telemarketers and offers strategies for avoiding them. Making any of these mistakes can be costly, waste your valuable time, and result in a lost sale or a dis-gruntled prospect.

In addition to avoiding the following common mistakes, always use your common sense with whatever issues arise as you deal with prospects and clients. Remember that, to ultimately close the sale, the prospect needs to trust and believe in you, your company, and the product/service you're selling. All of your actions, as they relate to each prospect, should somehow build upon that trust, either directly or indirectly.

Have a Daily, Weekly, and Monthly Plan

Without a plan in place, and an understanding of that plan, your efforts will be haphazard at best. Thus, you'll have difficulty achieving the maximum possible results from your efforts.

Knowing what you're trying to do and having a detailed plan for actually implementing that plan is crucial. Before kicking off your telemarketing efforts, know what you're trying to accomplish, what your sales goals are, and what needs to be done in order to achieve those objectives.

If, for example, you need to make 250 calls to new prospects in any given week in order to close 25 sales, that's 50 calls per day that must be made (assuming you're working Monday through Friday). Keeping in mind there will only be certain times of the day when you're most apt to reach a prospect by telephone, develop a schedule for yourself that allows you to make those 50 calls per day, but also address your other professional responsibilities.

Realize the Importance of Prioritizing Customers/Prospects

For the telemarketer, few things are more frustrating than making call after call to people who, for whatever reason, have no need or interest in what you're selling. Your time is valuable. Instead of wasting it, make sure you prequalify your prospects. As you do your preliminary research, ask:

- Who exactly is your target prospect?
- Does the prospect have a definite need for your product/service?
- What benefits does your product/service offer to your prospect?
- Can the prospect afford what you're selling?

Through research, you can target your telemarketing efforts to reduce time and resources wasted as a result of calling unqualified leads. Once you've gathered your prospect list, start by calling the prospects you believe are the most apt to purchase what you're selling. This determination is somewhat subjective, but if you know the answers to the previous questions you'll be able to make educated decisions when it comes to selecting prospects to contact.

Don't Drown in Paperwork!

It's easy to waste time and energy dealing with the plethora of paperwork that's often associated with telemarketing and making sales. Paperwork might include writing sales reports for your superiors, sending follow-up letters and information to prospects, keeping detailed notes of your sales calls, and insuring that your sales contracts are properly completed.

If not managed properly, paperwork can easily take valuable time away from the attention you need to focus on calling prospects and actually generating sales. Whenever possible, delegate your paperwork to a sales or administrative assistant. For the paperwork that needs to be completed by you personally, focus on streamlining that work as much as possible. One way to do this is by using database software, such as ACT! (*www.act.com*) to track contacts, and/or utilizing a computer to send form letters (with mail merge) to generate personalized correspondence, reports, and contracts. (See Chapter 13 for details about ACT! and other software packages.)

The best time to complete your mandatory paperwork is during the most nonproductive telemarketing hours—in other words, the times during the day when the people you're calling aren't available. This could be between 8 a.m. and 9 a.m. in the morning, during lunch, or late in the afternoon, for example. Keeping detailed notes and completing your paperwork in a timely manner is important, but this ancillary work should not interfere with your ability to make calls. After all, as a telemarketing professional, if you're not on the telephone, you're not making new sales.

Stay Focused Throughout Your Day

There will be times, for whatever reason, when your telemarketing efforts don't have the desired results. Thus, you could wind up making dozens of calls in a row, with no positive results. This can be a real morale buster. It's easy for telemarketers to get frustrated. Giving into that frustration, however, is a common error.

Especially when you're having a slow day, it's very easy to find reasons to delay making calls, take a long lunch, or leave at the end of the day earlier than you're supposed to. To achieve optimum success from your telemarketing efforts, you need to manage your day effectively.

For example, if you know you need to make 100 calls during the day in order to generate 10 sales, divide up your day so that during peak telemarketing times, you make 25 calls in a row. After that, take a short break before returning to work. Preplan your day so that, in the afternoon, you're not forced to spend several hours in a row making call after call with no break, simply because you didn't make enough calls in the morning or took an extra long lunch. Remember that the next call you make could result in a large sale.

Avoid Personal and Professional Time-Wasters

Throughout any given day, there are numerous things that can easily distract you from the task at hand: making calls. If you give into these distractions, your productivity will diminish. When you're telemarketing, don't allow yourself to get distracted.

Personal time-wasters to avoid (unless you're rewarding yourself with an earned break) include making personal telephone calls instead of calling prospects, taking frequent coffee breaks, chatting with coworkers, or surfing the Internet.

Professional time-wasters might include calling on unqualified prospects, being interrupted by coworkers knocking at your office door, trying to respond to unrelated mail and emails when you should be making calls, participating in unproductive meetings, and completing your paperwork during peak calling times.

Set time in your day to take breaks and deal with whatever personal and professional time-wasters and responsibilities are necessary, but don't allow these to impede upon your calling efforts.

Don't Ignore the 80-20 Rule

For almost any company, 80 percent of your business will come from a mere 20 percent of your customers. Thus, it's important to pay extra special attention to those customers who are responsible for the majority of your revenue. Allocate time during each day to keep in touch with your existing customers in order to better assess their needs, discover ways to increase revenues, or generate repeat business from already existing customers. In addition, use your established customer base as a source of referrals and as references when pursuing other clients. This is in addition to the time you spend making calls to new prospects in an effort to generate new business.

Don't Take Rejection Personally

Not every prospect you call will generate a sale. As a telephone sales professional, you're going to receive a tremendous amount of rejection—it's probably the most unpleasant part of the job. Some people will be extremely polite, whereas others will be rude or simply hang up the telephone. Remember that the rejection you experience has nothing to do with you personally.

There are many reasons why you might receive rejection, such as:

- You didn't properly prequalify your prospect.
- The prospect has no need or interest in your product/service.
- The prospect can't afford what you're offering.
- You called at a bad time.
- Your approach didn't capture the prospect's attention.

When you receive rejection, try to determine the cause of it, then make the necessary adjustments to your approach and pitch. If you called a prospect at a bad time, determine a better time to call (when you'll be able to obtain the full attention of the prospect). You may determine that your introduction or pitch isn't quickly capturing the interest of the prospect. Perhaps you need to rework your script or approach.

Not every prospect you call will have an immediate need for whatever you're selling. This, however, could change in the future. Even if a prospect isn't viable right now, try to determine if this will change in the future. Because circumstances constantly change, never burn your bridges with a prospect, even if at the moment things aren't looking good. Always act professionally so that, in the future, you can contact the prospect again and perhaps transform them into a customer.

Sometimes all it takes is persistence in order to transform a prospect into a customer. Keep in mind, however, that persistence and being a nuisance are two very different things. According to the National Sales Executive Association, 80 percent of all new sales are made after the fifth call to the same prospect. Thus, it's the persistent salespeople who achieve success.

This same research showed that 48 percent of all salespeople make just one call to a prospect. When the salesperson receives a negative response, he or she simply crosses that prospect off the list after the initial rejection. Likewise, 25 percent of all salespeople quit after the second call, and 12 percent call the same prospect three times then quit. Only 10 percent of telephone sales professionals keep calling on a qualified prospect (over time) until they succeed in landing a sale.

Avoid Setting Unrealistic Goals

During the planning stages for your telemarketing efforts, it is important to set realistic goals that are attainable. Although you don't want to make things too easy for yourself, setting unrealistic goals will increase your chances of getting frustrated and lower your morale.

If you have worked within your industry for a period of time, look at past performance and the performance of others within your company to determine realistic objectives. If, however, you are new to your industry, consult with others, such as managers within your organization or even people at other companies, to determine what would be considered realistic goals.

Evaluate your performance periodically and adjust your goals appropriately. The best way to set realistic goals is to keep accurate records of your activities. For example, on an ongoing basis, keep track of:

- The total number of calls you make each day.
- The number of calls to new prospects you make.

- The number of follow-up calls you make per day.
- The number of decision-makers you actually speak with each day.
- The number of gatekeepers, receptionists, and secretaries you speak with before reaching the decision-maker.
- The number of voice-mail messages you leave per day.
- The number of actual sales you close per day.

Using a pad of paper or an Excel spreadsheet, for example, you can easily chart this information and track it as you make your calls. Once you have these important statistics, you can determine your closing ratio by dividing the number of calls you made in a day with the number of sales made. You can then average this figure using a week's or a month's worth of data.

Don't Underestimate the Importance of Product/Service Knowledge

As a telemarketer, your perceived credibility is a crucial element in terms of your relationship with a prospect. If you're not knowledgeable about what you're selling, your credibility will be greatly diminished. Not only do you need to know everything possible about your product/service, but you also need to be able to present the appropriate information in a concise and easy to understand manner, plus be able to relate that information to the prospects own needs and desires.

In other words, simply knowing the raw facts and figures relating to your product isn't enough. You need to be able to explain how what you're offering can benefit the prospect. As you convey your knowledge, refrain from sounding as if you're simply reading a script or a product brochure. Part of your own preparation must involve spending time becoming thoroughly acquainted with whatever you're selling. You must also truly believe in your product/service in order to appear credible to the person you're speaking with on the telephone.

Remember that the prospect can neither see you nor the product/service you're selling. The person on the other end of the line must rely on what you say and how you say it in order to formulate his or her thoughts and decide whether to become a customer. Thus, if the prospect initially knows nothing about what you're selling, it'll be the knowledge you share with him or her that generates that all-important decision to buy.

Don't Waste Your Sales Efforts on Non-Decision-makers

Part of the prospect-qualification process involves quickly determining who the decision-maker is within an organization and getting that person on the telephone. It's too easy to spend time making an excellent sales presentation to someone, only to discover that he or she isn't the decision-maker.

To determine who the decision-maker is, do preliminary research and ask questions. Talk with the gatekeeper and briefly explain what you're offering. Then, ask who the appropriate person to speak with is. Even if you think you have the right person on the phone—the decision-maker—ask questions. Early in your conversation, you could ask, for example, "If you like what I have to offer, who else in your organization do we need to speak with in order to get approval and move forward?"

It's a common mistake for a telemarketer to expend the time and energy making his or her sales pitch to the wrong person within an organization. Another common mistake is talking to only one of the decision-makers, when the actual "buying" decision is made by business partners, multiple people within an organization, or a committee.

Chapter 13

Telemarketing Tools You Can Use

This chapter is all about helping you gather the additional tools, information, and resources to enhance your telemarketing efforts. Although you probably already have access to a telephone, assuming you'll be spending many hours per day making calls, you'd probably benefit greatly by adding a headset to that phone, for example, both for comfort and to free up your hands in order to take notes about your calls.

As you'll soon discover, technology can play a tremendous role in helping you become a more productive telesales representative. The companies and products described in this chapter are only a sampling of what's available.

Once you determine your specific needs, be sure to learn more about additional products and services by contacting one of the professional associations listed later in this chapter or using any Internet search engine. Using the Web, if you're looking for contact management software packages, aside from the ones described within this chapter, use the search phrase *contact management software* to learn about other products currently on the market.

Whether it's finding the perfect telephone headset or buying the best lead/prospect list to work from, everyone's needs and budgets are different. Use the information within this chapter as a starting point for obtaining tools and information, keeping in mind that the information provided here is an overview of the types of products and services available. Thus, if you read about a product or service that sounds useful, contact that company for additional information before making a purchase. The information here should not be considered an endorsement for any product or service.

The Perfect Environment

Creating a comfortable environment and gathering together the right collection of tools will make your telemarketing efforts a bit easier. Although you may be forced to work from a cubical in a noisy office or from a call center, there are still certain things you can do for yourself to make the environment more conducive to telemarketing. To begin, you want to eliminate all possible distractions and discourage interruptions. Next, focus on the comfort and functionality of your work environment.

Start with a comfortable chair. If you'll be sitting at your desk for hours at a time making call after call, it's important to have a chair that's comfortable and that offers lumbar support, for example. In addition to your primary sales tool, the telephone, other things you'll want in front of you while telemarketing might include:

- A computer, equipped with contact management software.
- A copy of your sales script and/or notes about your product/service.
- A mirror (so you can watch yourself work).
- Paper and a pen to write notes.

- A telephone headset. (Not only will this free your hands, some units offer noise cancellation technology, so you and your prospect will hear each other better if you're working from within a loud office.)
- Your lead/prospect list.

Contact Management Software

Telemarketing typically requires working from a lead/prospect list containing anywhere from a few dozen to thousands of prospects. Keeping track of whom you've called, what was discussed, what follow-up is required, and any details relating to that prospect can become a monumental task if not done efficiently.

Tapping the power of a contact management software package can make this process many times easier. Each of the contact management (also called personal information management) software packages described here continue to be used successfully by telesales and sales professionals to manage customers, leads, scheduling, and their telemarketing activities.

Which program you ultimately use should be based on your individual or company needs. By visiting the Website of each of these packages, you can often download a free 30-day trial or demo version of the software. Make sure the software package you choose offers the functionality you need before making your purchase.

Following are descriptions of several popular contact management programs currently on the market. These software packages are all compatible with Windows-based computers.

ACT!

Contact: (877) 386–8083

(888) 855–5222 (Corporate Licensing, 10 copies or more)

Website: *www.Act.com*

Price: $199.95 (single user)

For more than 15 years, ACT! has been the best-selling contact management solution for individuals, small businesses, and corporate workgroups within larger organizations. With more than four million individual users and 12,000 corporate accounts, ACT! is an easy-to-use product that assists sales people and business professionals in better managing and building relationships.

In addition to keeping track of contacts, ACT! includes full scheduling functionality, as well as sales tools and reporting capabilities. The software also integrates seamlessly with Microsoft Outlook, Palm OS handhelds, paper-based systems, and popular accounting products such as QuickBooks and Peachtree Accounting.

In terms of managing contacts, ACT! allows users to track complete contact information including name, company, phone numbers, address, Website, e-mail address, last meeting date, and much more. Multiple databases can be maintained, and lead/prospect lists from various sources can easily be imported into the software.

For each individual contact, ACT! allows you to store unlimited date- and time-stamped notes, so you can keep track of important conversations, commitments, and other pertinent information. In addition, ACT! allows you to:

- Manage all your customer information in one place.
- Utilize a full-featured database with more than 70 predefined fields. You can, however, totally customize fields to meet your specific needs.

- Tracks completed activities for each relationship and maintain a complete record of meetings held, letters sent, e-mails sent and received, calls completed, and more.

- No matter how large your contact database is, you can quickly find anyone or any detail quickly, using the instant Lookup and Keyword Search feature of the software.

- To share your information with others, you can generate printed phone lists, activity reports, relationship histories, sales summaries, and more, plus customize each type of report to meet your specific needs.

- In conjunction with each contact, you can attach, view, and edit important files (price lists, memos, letters, presentations, contracts, pictures, and so on) from within ACT!, giving you instant access to important documents.

For salespeople and telemarketing professionals, ACT! is one of the very best software applications on the market for contact management. The software is designed for individual use or for use within a small- to medium-sized organization. Large corporations, however, can utilize SalesLogix Sales software.

SalesLogix Sales

Contact: (800) 643–6400

Website: *www.saleslogix.com*

Price: Based on customer need/usage

SalesLogix Sales is a leading software-based solution for managing, forecasting, and reporting throughout all phases of the sales cycle. This software is designed to streamline the ancillary work associated with telemarketing, freeing up your time to actually make calls.

This software can be utilized by any type of sales professional, whether they're involved in field sales, telesales, partner channels, or sales via the Web. The software is designed to be used by dozens or even hundreds of users simultaneously and offers functionality to walk the salespeople though every step of the selling process, while at the same time tracking progress and providing detailed reports.

Maximizer

Contact: (800) 804–6299

Website: *www.maximizer.com*

Price: $189 (single user, downloadable version)

$199 (single user, CD version)

Two-, three-, four-, and five-user licenses available ($378–$995)

Maximizer is another leading sales and contact manager for individuals and small businesses. It offers a complete solution that incorporates contact management with sales opportunity management, communication, scheduling, reporting, a company library, and e-commerce. The software enables you to organize your time, manage your sales cycle, and improve customer tracking.

With Maximizer, you can easily market to and manage every customer and prospect, process and track every sale, and build and maintain relationships well after the initial sale has been made. The software is currently in use by more than one million users worldwide.

As does ACT!, for example, Maximizer allows you to simplify your daily tasks and manage an unlimited number of prospects and customers. You can also:

- ◆ Record and view a complete history of all customer interactions, including faxes, e-mails, and calls.

- Create unlimited user-defined fields within the database.

- Ensure accurate customer information through mandatory fields and duplicate record-checking.

- Create and save your own custom views and workspaces.

- Better track leads and manage sales by effectively tracking all opportunities, from lead to close.

- Manage an entire pipeline of opportunities from lead to close so you don't forget any lead or any sales step.

- Stay on track with customers and prospects by easily scheduling your time.

- Quickly schedule appointments and activities related to contacts, utilizing alarms and e-mail reminders. You can even prioritize task lists and schedule pop-up alarms that are active even when Maximizer is closed.

- Create letters, faxes, and e-mails stored under each contact for easy reference.

- Mail-merge contact information using built-in or custom templates, then create documents using the built-in Maximizer Word Processor, or use Microsoft Word or Corel WordPerfect.

- Share documents and sales collateral in the central company library.

- Access, view, and print more than 90 preformatted reports and graphs or create your own.

- Manage and reply to product inquiries.

Microsoft Outlook

Website: *www.microsoft.com/office/outlook*
Price: $109 (also comes bundled with Microsoft Office)

Although not specifically designed for salespeople or telemarketers, Outlook offers contact management functionality. This software provides a single, integrated solution for organizing and managing your digital communication tools, such as e-mail and instant messaging, along with all your day-to-day information, from calendars and contacts to task lists and notes.

Working seamlessly with Microsoft Office and some other Microsoft titles, Outlook 2002 gives you added control over e-mail, appointments, and contacts, helping you manage your time and tasks more effectively while making it easier to synthesize information and share it with others.

Telephone Equipment and Headsets

Assuming you already have your telephone system in place, this section focuses on some of the add-on tools you can use to make telemarketing easier. For example, a telephone headset will free up your hands and provide greater comfort if you spend hours at a time on the telephone.

According to a study conducted by H.B. Maynard & Associates, the use of a telephone headset allows users to work hands-free, which improves their productivity up to 43 percent. The American Association of Physical Therapists endorses the use of headsets, because they can reduce the risk of neck and back pain caused by holding or cradling a traditional telephone handset. Furthermore, a headset also provides better sound quality and will filter out background noise, which makes it easier to work in a noisy environment.

Telephone headsets can be connected to virtually any telephone or telephone system. There is a wide range of models available, including models that fit over one ear or both ears. The price of a single telephone headset ranges from $50 to $300, depending on the quality and functionality that's offered. You'll typically pay more, for example, for noise reduction and/or stereo sound.

In addition to offering a line-up of telephones and accessories, some of the companies that offer a full line of telephone headsets include:

- Andrea Electronics ((800) 442–7787 / *www.andreaelectronics.com*)
- Headsets.com, Inc. ((800) 450–7686 / *www.headsets.com*)
- Hello Direct, Inc. ((800) 444–3556 / *www.hello-direct.com*)
- Plantronics, Inc. ((800) 752–6876 / *www.plantronics.com*)
- Polycom, Inc. ((800) 765–9266 / *www.polycom.com*)

If you have a choice about the actual telephone equipment you'll be using, select a phone that offers the features you'll want to utilize, whether it's a caller-ID screen, hold button, speakerphone, headset jack (with built-in amplifier), redial button, mute button, and/or adjustable volume control for the handset. For example, Polycom's popular SoundPoint Pro SE-225 business telephone offers a wide range of functionality that a telesales professional will find desirable. Be sure to shop around for the equipment that offers the features you want at a price you can afford. Because many manufactures offer phone equipment for use at home or in business, prices tend to be extremely competitive.

Two other pieces of telephone equipment that are useful to a telemarketer are an auto-dialer and a recording device. As the name suggests, an auto-dialer takes each number from your lead list and dials it for you. This functionality is often incorporated into contact management software, specialized telemarketing software, or predictive dialer.

To maintain an audio record of your work and/or to later evaluate your skills as a telemarketer, it's an excellent idea to record some or all of your phone conversations. Keep in mind that there are specific laws in place relating to the recording of a phone conversation. To protect yourself, make sure the person you're speaking with understands that the call is being recorded.

Calls can be recorded using a standard cassette, micro-cassette, or digital voice recorder that gets connected to the telephone (or to your phone line). For less than $20, Radio Shack offers an accessory that connects any type of recorder (with a 1/4-inch microphone and ear jack) to a standard modular phone line. More complex equipment may be needed for office phone systems. Companies such as Hello Direct can help you determine the best way to record your inbound and outbound phone calls.

Another way to increase productivity is to utilize a predictive dialer. Use this technology for automated dialing. Predictive dialers work through a list of phone numbers (based on your list of prospects, for example), automatically dialing each one and screening out no answers, busy signals, and answering machines. The telemarketer only becomes involved in the process when a live person answers the phone.

Using this technology could allow you to enhance your telemarketing productivity by 150 to 400 percent. Predictive dialers are available in the form of a stand-alone unit or can be incorporated into a computer system that's running contact management software. The benefit of predictive dialers is that they can make many more calls in a much shorter period of time than if a person had to manually dial each phone number.

When the device encounters a busy signal or no answer, for example, it will automatically dial the number again later, without human intervention. Most systems can also keep track of an entire telemarketing campaign's progress, in real time. To learn more about predictive dialers, point your Web browser to one of the following:

- *www.the-resource-center.com/BOOKS/CTI/
  Predictive_dialing_fundamentals.HTM*
- *www.opc-marketing.com/predictivedialers.htm*
- *www.callcenters.com*

Using a package, called SalesStationPro, as an example, here's how predictive dialing works:

- Your computer rapidly dials numbers on your list until it gets an answer.

- When a live person gets on the line, you will hear a tone in your headset and you will be instantly connected to that person. Your marketing script and customer information will pop up on the computer screen immediately.

- If an answering machine or voice mail picks up, you can leave a prerecorded automated message. Once the message starts playing, your computer will begin dialing on another phone line.

- If you get an automated system, you can manually navigate through the phone system to find who you are trying to reach.

- You can update prospect information in ACT!, which is integrated into this system. Using ACT!, you can also schedule callbacks.

- From your computer, you can also send a fax or e-mail to the prospect instantly.

- When you receive inbound calls, SalesStationPro immediately displays the appropriate customer's information, through the use of Caller-ID.

- If you're not available, SalesStationPro can also function as a digital answering machine for incoming calls.

Sales Leads: Buying/Renting Lists

Telemarketing is all about calling prospects and closing sales. If you start off with a list that includes potential customers that are somewhat prequalified in that you know they fit your target demographic or meet specific criteria that you determine in advance, your chances of closing sales will increase dramatically.

There are many ways to obtain a lead list. One of the most common ways to acquire a list is to purchase one from a list broker. There are many types of lists that you can acquire, based on who you're trying to sell to. From a list broker, you can typically obtain a customized list, based on who you perceive your target customer to be. For example, there are lists comprised of Fortune 500 businesses, small businesses, home-based businesses, Yellow Page listings, and businesses within specific industries. You can also target specific geographic areas, companies with specific levels of sales, and individuals within companies who hold specific job titles. Lists can also be compiled based on SIC (Standard Industry Classification) codes. These codes are assigned to every type of business and industry for easy classification.

If you're trying to reach consumers, you can customize your list based on many things, such as:

- Age.
- Family/marital status.
- Geographic area.
- Income.
- Occupation.
- Political affiliation.
- Religion.
- Sex.
- Subscribers to specific publications.

- Type of housing (single-family home, apartment, condo, motor home, own/rent, and so forth).
- Credit rating and/or credit card information.

Typically, when you purchase a list from a broker, you'll pay on a per-lead basis. Some companies allow you to totally customize your list; others will sell you a pre-created list. Once you determine who you target customer is, be sure to shop around for lead lists. Rates vary greatly. The following are just a few of the list brokers that sell lead lists to telemarketers. Most of these companies will sell you a hard copy of the list (a printed version), or you can obtain the data in an electronic format and easily import it into contact management software such as ACT!.

When selecting a list, you need to know the following:

- Is the list information accurate, up-to-date, and "fresh?"
- Where did the data within the list originate from?
- How was it collected?
- Are the contacts on your list the type of people you're looking to reach through your telemarketing efforts? You may have to pay more for a targeted list, so the prospects will be more along the lines of your perfect potential customer. Your return on investment will then be higher, as will your rate of sales.

Some of the list brokers offer detailed Websites that allow you to browse and create customized lead lists online and then immediately purchase your list. All offer knowledgeable people who can help you reach your target customers using their list brokerage service to help you create your customized list.

Accurate Leads.com

Contact: (800) 685–4787

Website: *www.accurateleads.com*

This company allows you to create your list from its database of more than 16,000,000 businesses, 250 million individuals, and 120 million households. According to the company, its sources for its databases includes: Yellow Pages, White Pages, credit reports, SEC information, UUC data, government data (federal, state, county, city), business publications (newsletters, magazines, and major newspapers), mortgage data, new mover filings, credit bureau updates, and numerous proprietary sources.

USA Data

Contact: (800) 395–7707

Website: *usadata.com*

According to this company, "By using market research, you can identify the best population to target and then apply those criteria to filter from a compiled list. For example, if your target is males, aged 18–25, this selection criteria would be used to generate your prospect list. A response list is generated from customer response forms such as warranty cards and information request forms. Because it relies on people to supply their own information, it is not as complete as a compiled list. Therefore, when using a response list, there is risk of missing out on potential prospects."

Direct-Tel

Contact: (866) 204–3295

Website: *www.direc-tel.com/products_services.htm*

Direc-Tel offers a wide variety of lists and data hygiene services to accommodate your marketing needs, including:

- Consumer lists.
- Business lists.
- Specialty lists.
- New homeowner lists.
- Resident/occupant lists.

Go Leads

Contact: (402) 334–1824

Website: *www.goleads.com*

The unique thing about this service is that it offers its database of 12 million U.S. businesses for a flat monthly rate of $9.95. From this database, you can custom create lead lists based on your needs.

Long Distance Telephone Service

Whether you're making calls from home, a small business, or a large corporation, when it comes to making local, regional, or long distance (state-to-state) calls, your options are plentiful in terms of the phone company or carrier you use. It's important to shop around for the best rates in order to keep your costs down.

You'll often find that the smaller long distance resellers offer more competitive rates than the larger carriers, such as AT&T or Sprint. A long distance reseller is a company that purchases blocks of long-distance telephone service in bulk at a reduced price and then sells the long-distance to consumers at a rate below what they would normally pay.

Once you have begun making your calls, you'll quickly be able to determine the average amount of time you spend per call. If the average call is three minutes, and you're spending $.15 per minute on long distance phone charges, that's a cost of $.45 per call. Add to this the cost of labor, basic phone service, the purchase fee for your prospect list, and so on, and the costs add up quickly. Thus, finding the most competitive call rates will help your bottom line. Galaxy Internet Services (www.gis.net), for example, offers highly competitive long distance rates and reliable service to small, medium, and large businesses.

Using any Internet search engine, use the search phrase *long distance service* to begin shopping for the best rates. Be sure to read the fine print, however, when you start seeing deals that seem too good to be true.

SmartPrice.com (*www.SmartPrice.com*) is a free service that helps you find the best deals in long distance. Answer a few questions and the site will find the best options that meet your needs.

Other Resources:
Professional Associations, Magazines,
Newsletters, and Websites

Following are professional organizations, magazines, newsletters, and Web sites that telemarketing professionals will find offer an abundance of useful information:

◆ **American Marketing Association** ((800) AMA–1150/ *www.ama.org*). The AMA has more than 40,000 members worldwide, in 82 countries, with nearly 400 chapters throughout North America and Canada. It is the only organization that provides direct benefits to marketing professionals in both business and education and serves all levels of marketing practitioners, educators, and students. Membership includes a subscription to *Marketing News,* the AMA's biweekly magazine, which covers ongoing shifts in the industry: Globalization, Technology and Legislative/ Regulatory/Economic developments. *Marketing News* keeps members on the leading edge of marketing.

- **American Teleservices Association, Inc.** ((877) 779–3974/ *www.ataconnect.org*). This organization represents the call centers, trainers, consultants, and equipment suppliers that initiate, facilitate, and generate telephone, Internet, and e-mail sales, service, and support. Call centers offer traditional and interactive services that support the e-commerce revolution, provide specialized customer service for Fortune 500 companies, and generate annual sales of more than $500 billion. The ATA represents members' interests by advocating on Capitol Hill and in statehouses nationwide, providing advanced professional education opportunities, defending the teleservices industry in the public realm, and acting as the industry's information clearinghouse. A free online-based newsletter, *E-Connections,* is available from the Website.

- **Call Center Magazine** ((847) 588–0682/ *www.callcentermagazine.com*). This publication provides in-depth and unbiased product and strategic information that executives responsible for improving customer relations and retention through call centers rely upon to make purchasing decisions on the hardware, software, and services critical to their success. The magazine is read by call center managers, IT managers, and other professionals who are involved in the operation of call centers and customer support departments. Through in-depth product guides, case studies, and special features, the publication keeps its readers informed on the latest developments in call center technology, management, and operations. Monthly features include case studies, new product reviews, outsourcing and site location features, special columns that offer coverage of emerging trends, and research highlights. Subscriptions are free to qualified people.

- **Call Center News Service** ((323) 663–3082/ *www.callcenternews.com*). This newsletter is published biweekly and covers the products, services, and techniques used in running call centers. Price: $199 per year.

- **Direct Marketing Association** ((212) 768–7277/ *www.the-dma.org*). The DMA is the oldest and largest trade association for users and suppliers in the direct, database, and interactive marketing fields. Founded in 1917, its 5,000-plus members include catalog companies, direct mailers, teleservices firms, Internet marketers, and other at-distance marketers from every consumer and business-to-business segment—both commercial and nonprofit—as well as companies that provide supplies and services to marketers.

- **Discount Long Distance Digest** (*www.thedigest.com*). This is a free online newsletter for the long distance telephone industry that covers issues that affect long distance carriers and resellers, long distance agents, and consumers. Topics covered include long distance rates and calling plans; competitive local telephone service; payphones; long distance agent and affiliate programs; 800 toll-free and 900 pay-per-call service; Voice Over Internet Protocol (VOIP); wireless, cellular, and PCS service; dial-around services; prepaid phone cards; long distance slamming; and much more.

- **Help Desk Institute** ((800) 248–5667/ *www.helpdeskinst.com*). Founded in 1989, HDI is the world's largest membership association for help desk and support center professionals. HDI is member-focused and remains vendor-neutral in its efforts to facilitate open, independent networking and information-sharing within the HDI association network. HDI has more than 7,500 members worldwide and more than 50 active U.S. chapters. Ninety percent of the Fortune 500 are members of HDI. In addition to HDI's commitment to membership initiatives, HDI develops and produces its own open standard certification program and offers its certification training through online offerings and a network of authorized trainers. HDI also sponsors its own annual conference and expo and publishes *SupportWorld* magazine, *Industry Insider* e-newsletter, and *The Muns Report* e-newsletter. HDI also publishes several surveys, research reports, and white papers and maintains an extensive knowledge base on the HDI Website.

- ◆ **Society of Consumer Affairs Professionals in Business** ((703) 519–3700/*www.socap.org*). Membership is open to all professionals who are in some way responsible for creating and maintaining customer loyalty: vice presidents, directors, managers, and supervisors with responsibilities for consumer affairs, customer service, customer relationship management, inbound call centers, market research, information systems integration, sales and marketing, database management, new business development and operations. As customer-driven management techniques expand in popularity and the emphasis on retaining customers becomes more critical to business success, SOCAP provides the tools needed for corporations to reach their goal of maximum customer loyalty, excellent customer service, and value-added innovations. SOCAP membership is composed of close to 3,000 corporate consumer affairs/customer service professionals, representing more than 1,500 companies. Most of these companies are listed in the *Fortune/Forbes 1000*. The organization's fax-on-demand system ((703) 549–4886) allows people to retrieve information on membership, chapters, upcoming conferences, job opportunities, *Customer Relationship Management* magazine, Resource Center bookstore, exhibits, and more.

Chapter 14

THE EXPERTS SPEAK OUT

Each chapter of *Top Telemarketing Techniques* has taken one aspect of telemarketing and provided the information you need to be successful. Now that all of the components of being a successful telesales professional have been explained, this chapter wraps everything up with a group of highly successful telemarketing executives sharing their advice and experiences from the real world.

Within these interviews, the experts share their personal techniques that have been successful, offer advice for avoiding the mistakes they've made, and provide the strategies they believe will help you to achieve your goals as a telemarketer.

You'll notice that, although each person specializes in telemarketing within a different industry or works as a consultant to companies in a wide range of industries, their actual telephone sales techniques and strategies are often similar. These people simply adapt their skills, knowledge, and sales experience to suit whatever product or service they're selling.

In addition to learning from these telemarketing experts, study the work of top performers at your company (both coworkers and superiors) and learn their techniques for successfully selling the products or services you will be selling once you kick off your own telemarketing efforts. Until you begin gaining your own firsthand experience, learning from other successful people can be extremely beneficial in this line of work.

Tom Morrill

President and CEO
Actegy Incorporated
Phone: (978) 557–0182
Website: *www.actegy.com*

In this interview, Tom Morrill shares his more than 16 years worth of telemarketing and sales experience, as well as information he has learned in the years he's been the president and CEO of Actegy, Inc., a sales consulting practice that enables high technology companies to acquire, retain, and grow profitable customers by building or refocusing their inside and outside sales organizations. Actegy (a name coined by combining the words *action* and *strategy*) helps its clients drive results by providing industry experienced sales executives as consultants and arming them with proven tools, models, methods, and programs to help their clients achieve telemarketing success.

Q. What is the most important thing a company or individual needs to understand before starting any type of telemarketing effort?

A. "Any company, no matter what its size, must first understand its value proposition in the marketplace. It needs to know who its target customer is; what problem its product or service can solve and how; and what benefits its product or service will offer to its customers. With this information in mind, the telemarketer needs to understand the clients buying behavior so they can determine whether or not inside sales [telemarketing] is appropriate. You need to make sure your efforts fit nicely into your target customers' buying cycle. By clearly understanding the customer's buying behavior and what the customer requires during their purchase cycle, you can easily determine how to successfully utilize inside sales. It's all dictated by the customer. It's been said that the cheapest channel for reaching the customer is always the best channel, but that's not always the case. It depends on what the customer requires to facilitate their procurement process. If you're able to meet your customer's needs, you're more apt to make sales."

Q. What are the key skills a telemarketer should have to achieve success?

A. "People with a specific personality type tend to have greater success in any type of sales position. If someone is emotionally and psychologically equipped to be good at making sales, [he or she] can learn the specific skills needed to be a good telesales professional. Someone who is more apt to be a good telemarketer has the natural ability to communicate with others, both face-to-face and over the phone. They also have the ability to avoid taking rejection personally and the ability to handle basic negotiations. Absolute focus, organization skills, discipline, and determination are also key traits someone needs to be successful in this field."

Q. Based on your experience, what do the day-to-day responsibilities of a telemarketer entail?

A. "This will vary greatly from job to job. There are many different types of telemarketing and telesales jobs. Typically, telemarketer[s] start their workday in the morning by getting totally organized and mentally preparing before getting on the phone. This includes getting their prospect or lead list together so they know exactly who they'll be calling that day. Next, the telemarketer should set their daily goals. I like to make groups of similar calls. What I mean by this, is that if you're making cold calls and follow up calls that day, group the cold calls together. You can group together your calls by location, the title of the person you're trying to reach, the product or service you're selling, by type of target customer, by type of industry, or by zip code. Mentally, this will help you fine-tune your message and easily carry your findings from call to call. It's also easier to gauge success levels. Once the day is planned and the objectives have been set, it's time to start making calls. Time also needs to be allocated in the day to handle all administrative tasks. After every call, chances are there will be something that needs to be done, whether it's sending out information, writing down detailed notes about what was discussed, creating and sending a proposal, or setting a follow up time. When planning your day, you need to allocate ample time to handle all of these tasks.

"Entry-level telemarketers will usually have their day structured for them. They'll sit down, plug in their telephone headset and start making calls from a predetermined call list using a preplanned sales pitch or script. Many call centers are equipped with predictive dialers and the low-level telemarketers are at the mercy of this technology in terms of their ongoing calling activities. Higher level telemarketers have a lot more latitude and control over their day, who they call and what they say during their calls."

Q. Having acquired so many years of telemarketing experience, what's your favorite part of the job?

A. "People who are emotionally and psychologically equipped to be good salespeople can transform the work they do telemarketing into a fun and rewarding experience. For those people who aren't cut out for this type of work, it can be as painful as root canal without Novocain. I classify myself as being an overachiever. For me, the best thing about telemarketing was always getting the appointment, when my job included prequalifying prospects and making appointments on the phone, then going out on face-to-face sales calls. For me, telemarketing is all about taking a tactical approach. You set short-term goals for yourself and then you determine what you need to do that day to achieve or exceed those goals."

Q. What's the biggest benefit of pursuing a telemarketing career?

A. "At many companies, telemarketing positions are entry-level. You can work your way up into other sales positions that have more lucrative pay, once you gain experience and knowledge about the product or service you're selling and the industry you are working in. For an experienced telemarketer or telesales professional, you can have incredible earning potential. I am in my early 40s right now, but I got into sales when I was 21. I still use the same skills I learned early on, but with time, I have mastered those skills and expanded upon them. Telemarketing offers many opportunities."

Q. What is your least favorite aspect of telemarketing and how do you deal with it?

A. "There are days when you'll make cold calls all day long, but receive no positive results.

"Those are the times when this job can be frustrating, no matter how good you are. It's important to realize, however, that telemarketing is a numbers game. I remember one day several years ago when I had a really bad day. I made hundreds of calls with no positive results. The very next morning, however, I made one of the largest sales I had ever made to date. Instead of getting depressed that you're getting a lot of 'no's,' you just have to focus on how many more 'no's' you'll need until you get a 'yes.' After about 30 days in any telemarketing job, you'll be able to do the math and track pretty accurately how many 'no's' you need to receive for every 'yes.' Receiving rejection is tough, but if you focus on your numbers and stats, you'll always know the next 'yes' is only a certain number of calls away, and that should keep you coming back for more."

Q. What are some of the challenges involved with making cold calls?

A. "For many people, the biggest challenge is actually picking up the phone to make a call, because they're afraid of rejection. Once you overcome that, dealing with rejection can be a challenge. You have to realize that even if someone is rude to you, it's not personal. You just move on. Another challenge is setting goals at the beginning of the day and then working hard and staying motivated until you achieve those goals. One pitfall people run into is that they quit early and get into the habit of not achieving their daily goals."

Q. When someone actually begins making cold calls to prospects, what are some of the most common objections he or she will encounter, and what strategies have you discovered to overcome them?

A. "It's important to understand there is a difference between an objection and a condition. An objection can be overcome, but a condition can not. An example of a condition is when a prospect tells you, 'We're going bankrupt and we have no money.' You can use all of the closing techniques in the world, but if the prospect has no money, they can't make a purchase. It's your job to accept what can not be changed and move on.

"There are four steps to handling any objections. You need to clarify the objection and make sure you understand what the prospect is objecting to. Second, empathize. Make it clear that it's okay for the prospect to feel the way they do. The third step is to offer a solution or an alternative. Finally, the last step is saying something like, 'Does this make sense to you?' and then try to close the sale."

Q. What are some of your best strategies for keeping a sales pitch fresh when you're forced to repeat it over and over throughout the day?

A. "The easiest thing to do is change the pitch. For example, try using a different close or present your solution in a different way. If you're forced to do the same pitch over and over, have one of your associates or supervisors listen to you periodically to make sure you're maintaining the appropriate inflections in your voice. Being able to close a sale involves being able to understand the circumstances on the other side of the phone. You need to understand how what your organization is offering aligns with the prospect's needs. When you understand both sides, you'll become far better at communicating with your prospects. Always try to envision what you sound like to the person you're speaking with."

Q. Have you devised any particular techniques for closing a sale?

A. "There are many strategies you can implement when trying to close a sale. It all depends on the product or service you're selling and what the needs of your prospect are. I always recommend incorporating a trial close into a pitch. Say something like, 'Can you see how this would be a benefit?' Try to gain confirmation that the prospect agrees with your recommendation. You can also try 'the alternative close' by asking, 'Would this be good, or would you prefer this alternate option?' There are thousands of closing techniques. I suggest keeping your technique as simple at possible. After you've made your pitch, one simple technique that works well is to ask for the sale. Remember, if your prospect is not ready to buy or in a position to buy, no closing technique is going to work. Whether you're selling to consumers or business-to-business, create a sense of urgency in your sales pitch to help facilitate a close."

Q. On an ongoing basis, what can someone do to continue to hone their telemarketing skills?

A. "Subscribe to a few of the many telemarketing-oriented periodicals out there. Whenever possible, attend sales or telesales skills training seminars or programs. On a weekly or biweekly basis, spend some time studying what your successful coworkers are doing in order to get different ideas. It's also a good idea to ask your supervisor or boss to periodically listen in on a few of your calls and seek out their feedback. I often record some of my sales calls and analyze them later."

Q. One of the things you teach your clients is to overcome sales performance barriers. What does this mean, and how does it apply to telemarketing?

A. "Sales performance barriers can impact five different areas that relate to actually making sales. First, you want to make sure you have an accurate and achievable plan in place. If your overall telemarketing plan is flawed, you will never achieve your goal. Second, as an individual telemarketer, are you effective? If you are not effective in your execution, that is a barrier to making sales. Third, determine if your process is efficient. If you have too much paper on your desk, you're not taking advantage of technology to automate some of your paperwork. If you're disorganized, you're not maximizing your efficiency and that costs you valuable time. Fourth, if you're utilizing technology, is it enabling you to make sales, or is it disabling you due to complexity or lack of the appropriate features or customization? Finally, make sure there are no barriers in your sales pipeline. For example, are you moving prospects appropriately from step to step along your sales cycle in a timely manner?"

Barry Maher

President
Barry Maher & Associates
Phone: (760) 962–9872
Website: *www.BarryMaher.com*

Selling Power magazine declared, "To his powerful and famous clients, Barry Maher is simply the best sales trainer in the business." Whether as a speaker, author, or consultant, Barry is hired to get results. Over the years, Barry has helped hundreds of clients, of all sizes and from a wide range of industries, to improve productivity, sales, and ultimately their bottom line. Barry's career as a salesperson began at age 6, when he responded to an ad in a comic book and began selling greeting cards door to door. At age 16, his first real job was selling magazine subscriptions door-to-door. Since then, he has sold everything from theater tickets to advertising opportunities to securities using the telephone. He's been working as a sales and telesales consultant since 1985.

Q. What do you like most about telemarketing as opposed to other methods of selling?

A. "It's wonderful. If I were to make in-person sales calls, on the best day, I might only be able to participate in 10 meetings. With telesales, I can use that same amount of time and contact dozens, perhaps hundreds of prospects. Sales is a numbers game, and you can achieve far greater numbers using the telephone. Thus, you'll have much less unproductive downtime. To stay motivated, I try to stay focused on my customers and try to determine what needs they have, even before they realize them. Satisfying the customer's needs, solving a problem and at the same time making a sale as a result is an incredible feeling. I find it exciting to continuously work my way to the top position in the sales force I'm working with."

Q. How important is a telemarketer's attitude?

A. "It's critical. If you go into a call expecting the prospect to buy, they'll pick up on that. The prospect will realize, based on your attitude, that you believe you are offering them a truly good deal and they'll tend to believe it. The attitude is communicated by what you say, how you say it, and the emotions you convey over the phone. How you deliver your sales pitch is critical."

Q. What are some of your best strategies for keeping a sales pitch fresh when you're forced to repeat it over and over throughout the day?

A. "The primary responsibility of the telemarketer is to create an excitement and interest in a product or service. It's too easy for this job to turn into rote and thus become drudgery for the telemarketer. There are a lot of things a telesales professional can do to maintain their own excitement. I recommend keeping a mirror or your desk so you can watch yourself while making calls and gauge your level of excitement. I also recommend standing up, using a telephone headset and pacing around a bit when selling over the telephone."

Q. What are some of the mistakes you see novice telesales professionals make?

A. "They're afraid of failure and rejection. You can't be afraid of potential negatives as they relate to the product or service you're selling. It's possible to use a negative as a positive. For example, if I were to call a prospect to offer them my consultation services, one objection I might receive is that my fees are too high. I might respond, 'You bet they're expensive! Why do I charge so much? Because I can. My clients are willing to pay my rates because of the results I generate. Can you find someone to work with you for less? Definitely. But do you really think those people would be charging less if they could charge more? They charge less because that's what they're worth and that's what their clients are willing to pay for the services they receive.' If there are negatives, I recommend getting them out on the table in a positive way. You need to be able to sell the product or service to yourself first, before you can convince someone else to buy it."

Q. When someone actually begins making cold calls to prospects, what are some of the most common objections they'll encounter, and what strategies have you discovered to overcome them?

A. "There are several challenges. Getting past the gatekeeper is a challenge for everyone. Once you get through to the right person, you need to generate immediate interest. Over the years, I have used more than 50 different ways to get through the gatekeepers. One method that works well is to make the assumption that I will get through the gatekeeper by stating, 'Hi, is Bill there? This is Barry.' I won't ever say this is 'Barry Maher.' When the gatekeeper says, 'Barry who?', I respond by saying, 'Barry Maher. I need to speak with Bill.' That usually gets me through right away, because I project the assumption that I will get through to the person I am calling. If I sound unsure and believe I'm not going to get through, I won't. If, for example, you mispronounce the person's name or make it clear you have no clue who you're calling, you won't get past the gatekeeper. As opposed to trickery, I find the simplest approaches for getting through to the decision-maker always work best. Another method that works well is to send a letter or fax first, then make a call stating you're following up on the information you sent.

"In terms of generating the immediate interest once you get through to the decision-maker, you need to use an interest-creating remark right at the start. This remark will depend on the product or service you're selling. A good telesales operation will develop several good interest-creating remarks and recommend or insist that their telesales force use them. I remember I was once selling advertising for a publication in a college town. The line I used was, 'I have 10,000 students located a few blocks away from your business. Are you interested in reaching them?' I used this line before I mentioned I was selling advertising space in a college bookstore magazine. If you provide too much information too quickly, the prospect could decide they don't want what you're selling. If I said I was selling advertising space in a college bookstore magazine right at the start of the call, my prospects would have hung up right away. Your success will depend on the structure of your presentation."

Q. How do you overcome the common objections you receive when telemarketing?

A. "There are many different types of objections you're sure to encounter. The price objection is probably the most common. One way to overcome this objection is to change the scale. In other words, if I say the price is $3,200 per year, someone might respond that it's a lot of money. If you break that down to how much your product or service is per hour, per day or per month, the cost becomes more reasonable. That same $3,200 per year is really only $61.53 per week or less than $8.75 per day, for example.

"Another thing you can do is play up the high price point early on. Make the person want the product or service, but worry he or she won't be able to afford it. I make my whole sales pitch and never mention price. I wait for the prospect to ask. If the prospect doesn't ask the price, I have not done my job to convince them they want what I'm selling. When they ask about the price, I sometimes respond, 'It's a boat load' or 'It's a lot of money, but worth every penny." This makes the prospect envision a high price and wish they could afford it. I then tell them the price, and repeat the fact that it's a lot of money, even though I know it is well within the prospect's budget. I want the prospect to immediately think, 'Hey, that's not a lot of money. I can afford that.' I always suggest the most expensive package possible, knowing this will be the start of a negotiation process. If I recommend large, but I become sure the prospect won't buy what I just offered, I offer another less expensive recommendation. I often have a handful of fallback recommendations."

Q. How do you stay motivated throughout the day when telemarketing?

A. "I collect 'no's' knowing that after reaching a certain number of them, I'll get the 'yes' I am looking for. I know that telemarketing is purely a numbers game. The most successful salespeople are the ones who hear the most 'no's.' The more 'no's' someone receives, the more sales they'll ultimately make. I keep detailed records of my calls and develop daily goals for myself. I know how many calls it takes me to get a lead, how many calls it takes to reach a decision-maker, and how many calls I need to make to get a sale. I know, on average, if I make 200 calls, I'll achieve a certain level of sales. The trick is to keep the process fun and interesting for yourself and your prospects. Use your sense of humor. Laughter is an excellent sales tool, especially on the phone."

Q. On an ongoing basis, what do you do to keep honing your telemarketing skills?

A. "I keep selling. I read everything I can about sales, and I talk to as many other salespeople as I can find. Most of what I learn comes from watching other salespeople work and by interacting with prospects and customers myself. After I make each call, I think about what I could have done better or how I could have worded something better. I then apply these changes to my next calls, so my pitch is always evolving. Be sure to learn from your mistakes."

David English

President
Technology Sales Leads
Phone: (617) 426–4510
(877) 241–8546
Website: *www.tsleads.com*

Technology Sales Leads (TSL) was founded in April 1999 to provide enterprise prospecting and telemarketing services to technology companies worldwide. TSL is a growing company with a multilingual staff and offices in the United States, the United Kingdom, Africa, India, and Ireland. Its clients include some of the fastest-growing software companies in Europe and North America, as well as "blue chip" technology companies. The company's focus involves developing high quality sales leads for technology and professional services companies. Through its telemarketing division, The Contact Company, TSL provides traditional telemarketing services. Prior to cofounding TSL, David worked for IBM North America in Boston and Chicago.

Q. Your specialty involves helping companies find prospects for their product or service. How do you do this?

A. "We work with our clients to pinpoint the very best prospects for the product or service they're selling. In addition to finding the prospects, we'll determine who the key decisions-makers are and supply the client with a detailed and highly select list of prequalified prospects, including the names, titles, and contact information of the decision-makers. We consider what we do to be the first step in a high-end telemarketing approach, because as opposed to targeting larger, mass markets, we help our clients reach very well-defined or niche markets. Thus, when a telemarketer uses a list prepared by us, they spend less time finding qualified buyers and decision-makers and more time using their expertise actually selling to the appropriate people.

"When a new client comes to us, we spend a lot of time analyzing what they offer and making sure we develop the right list of prospects for them to sell to. We believe that the better the prospect list the client works with, the faster and easier they'll be able to generate sales. Once we pinpoint the prospects and develop a list, we strategize with the client to develop their pitch and fine tune the best sales messages."

Q. How do you choose the best prospects for your clients?

A. "This all depends on the product or service that will be sold. Sometimes, defining a target market is easy and straightforward. Sometimes it's more complex. In addition to analyzing the product or service, we look at who the customers have been in the past and what those customers have in common. We also pay attention to economic factors, to make sure that the prospects our client will be targeting can afford what's being offered.

"Our specialty is developing lead lists for our clients from scratch. We use many different sources, including list brokers, to begin compiling our lists. This tends to be a more expensive way for a company to develop a lead list, but the positive results support the additional up-front expense. It's better for a telemarketer to utilize a list of prequalified prospects where all of the information is accurate, than it is for them to use a list with errors, that's outdated, or that contains prospects that don't need the product or service being sold."

Q. What common mistakes do telemarketers make when developing a prospect list?

A. "They may pinpoint appropriate companies to contact, for example, but they spend time trying to sell to a prospect's satellite offices when the buying decisions for the entire company are made from the corporate office. This is a common mistake that wastes the telemarketer's resources and time. It's important to make sure the prospects you're reaching are, in fact, qualified to buy your product or service and that as the telemarketer, you have a functional prospect management strategy in place. This typically means using a specialized database software package. We use our own proprietary software for our clients, but in terms of the off-the-shelf packages, we haven't found one in particular that outshines the others. What's more important is to insure the telemarketer uses a software package with the functionality they need. It's vital that prospects don't get lost in a telemarketing company's sales cycle.

"If a company is using telemarketing to supplement a field sales force, it's important for all of the reps to have access to the prospect database. The field reps should be able to access the information with a laptop computer, for example. Everyone should have access to all of the information they need. It's also important that the prospect management software be able to capture information in an efficient way."

Q. Traditional list brokers offer a wide range of options to telemarketers. What should a telemarketer look for when purchasing a lead list?

A. "There are a lot of questions to ask to insure that you're purchasing a list you will best be able to utilize. For example, you want to know how the names are collected, how up-to-date the information is, and how accurate the information is. One of the biggest problems with buying an off-the-shelf list is that a high percentage of the information may be outdated or inaccurate. If you have a 30-percent inaccuracy rate on a list you purchase, that represents a lot of lost time and effort on your part as you begin your telemarketing efforts. One common mistake is that telemarketers buy the cheapest list they can find. This may or may not be the best strategy, because the quality of the list will impact your success once you actually start telemarketing. The more customized and qualified the leads are on your list, the better results you'll have. The initial cost related to buying higher quality names will offer a much better return later on.

"As the telemarketer, if you do your homework and pinpoint exactly who you're trying to reach before contacting a list broker, you're more apt to purchase a list with good leads; prospects who have a want to need for your product or service. I always recommend that before spending a fortune on an expensive list, you pay a small amount for a test list. Call those prospects on the test list to insure it has the quality of data you need. This might mean purchasing a few hundreds names at first as opposed to thousands."

Q. How important is starting your telemarketing efforts with a good lead list?

A. "This is important, but several other aspects of telemarketing are equally important. The quality of your sales pitch and the skills of the telemarketers themselves are important for making sales. Many components have to come together nicely to achieve success."

Carla Meine

Founder and President
O'Currance Teleservices, Inc.
Phone: (801) 736–0500
Website: *www.ocurrance.com*

O'Currance Teleservices is one of the country's leading providers of telemarketing services, providing inbound and outbound sales, order processing, and other services to its clients. *Telemarketing Magazine* recently named O'Currance Teleservices as the second-fastest-growing telemarketing company in the nation.

Founded in 1994, O'Currance Teleservices has led the way in the development of Web-based virtual offices and remote telesales agents. Currently, more than 80 percent of the company's workforce is enabled to work from home offices. O'Currance's innovative approach to handling inbound calls from virtual offices is fast becoming an industry standard and is one of its many keys to success. The company is headquartered in Salt Lake City and has a staff of 196 full-time sales agents and supervisors, but it expands its part-time force as needed in order to handle specific projects for its clients.

Before founding O'Currance, Carla was the vice president of operations for Morris Air, where she supervised more than 800 agents in the company's reservation center, as well as its human resource department, flight attendants, sales associates, ticket agents, and airport operations.

In this interview, Carla discusses the work of an average inbound telemarketer (someone who responds to incoming calls as a result of a prospect dialing a toll-free phone number to place an order after seeing an advertisement or reading a catalog, for example).

Q. How does O'Currance Teleservices differ from other inbound call centers?

A. "I founded this company almost 10 years ago. At the time, we were one of the first to utilize technology to allow us to have remote telesales agents. This means our inbound telemarketers can work from home, but be remotely connected to our system via the Internet. At the time, we were one of the first companies to utilize this technology. The results have been vastly improved productivity, because our agents can work from their home and have flexible schedules.

"I want my company to be the leading call center in the world. Instead of hiring entry-level telemarketers, I hire highly skilled sales people. I tend to hire middle-aged people with a lot of experience and a college education. I believe that if I hire great people, I'll have a great company. This is part of the equation. The other part is providing those people with the best technology and most powerful sales tools available. This combination leads to success. When someone works from home, they use a computer that's connected directly to our system. The inbound callers have no clue they are calling a telemarketer who is working from home, because everything happens exactly the same way as it does for the telemarketers working directly from our call center.

"Unlike other call centers that are staffed by inexperienced high school and college students, at O'Currance Teleservices, we offer a higher-end inbound telemarketing service to our clients, because our staff is experienced. As a result, we offer our telemarketers a commission on every sale they make in addition to their hourly salary. This allows for much higher income potential for them, even if they work part-time."

Q. The concept of remote telemarketing agents was new when you founded your company. How has this concept been adapted into the telemarketing industry since?

A. "At the time O'Currance Teleservices was founded, what we were doing and much of the technology we used was proprietary. These days, there are many companies and call centers that utilize similar technology to allow telemarketers to work from remote locations. We still, however, utilize proprietary technology in terms of how our systems actually work. For example, we've created what we call the 'IntelliScript' system, which automatically customizes the sales script the telemarketer reads, based on responses from the customer. We've also developed our own scheduling tools to manage our remote agents. Because we have these specialized, technology-based tools, we're often still ahead of what our competitors offer in terms of call center services."

Q. As an inbound call center, what types of clients do you cater to?

A. "Several of our clients produce television infomercials. We handle their inbound order taking and customer service. Other clients utilize more traditional TV, radio, or print advertising where customers respond by calling a toll-free number, which gets routed to our call center. We also have clients who use us for dedicated projects. This means that we hire and train a dedicated group of agents who do nothing but respond to calls for that specific client. These agents go through more extensive training about the product or service they'll be selling. These telemarketing services are often utilized by companies selling higher priced products or services, where the telemarketer needs to be extremely knowledgeable and have excellent sales skills to be able to close the sale. The people we hire for this type of job are different from the telemarketers who might handle incoming calls from dozens of different companies at any given time and switch from script to script as they deal with those calls."

Q. When you look to hire new inbound telemarketers, what do you look for?

A. "Number one, I look for people with previous sales experience. Applicants can apply for employment directly from our Website and use what we call our 'Predictive Index.' This is an online survey that helps us find the right applicants based on their skills. During the interviewing process, we audition telemarketers to see how well they read prepared scripts."

Q. What are the day-to-day responsibilities of an inbound telemarketer?

A. "Their main responsibility, after they've gone through our 30-day training program, is to be available during the times they're scheduled to work. Once they log into the system to work, whether it's from home or from our call center, they begin taking incoming calls, with the goal of selling a particular product or service. The IntelliScript they will follow for that product or service will appear on their computer screen. Because we are a call center working with many clients, most of the time our telemarketers are required to follow the script we provide verbatim, because we know that it works. For special dedicated projects, the telemarketers are given some latitude. The telemarketer also needs to deal with customer service-type calls from people who have questions about products they've already purchased. [Because] we operate seven-days-a-week, 24-hours-per-day, we hire people to work during a wide range of shifts. The biggest drawback to working for an inbound telemarketing call center is the scheduling. Sometimes, we won't find out until Friday afternoon that one of our clients has their infomercials running that weekend, so we need to have our telemarketers on call to work with little notice, even on weekends. When someone does outbound telemarketing, they have some control over when the calls are actually made. With inbound telemarketing, we have no clue when people are going to respond to an ad, infomercial, or place an order after reading a catalog."

Q. What are some of the benefits of an inbound telemarketing job?

A. "In a perfect situation, the inbound telemarketer can work from home, have a flexible work schedule, earn a commission on the sales they make, and not have to deal with the stresses and challenges of traditional outbound telemarketing, which involves cold calling. Many experienced telemarketers appreciate being able to work from home because a typical call center environment can be very noisy and hectic, which makes it difficult to concentrate. Someone who handles inbound calls has an advantage because the prospect calls them and already has an interest in the product or service. Although remote telesales job opportunities are still somewhat rare, more and more companies around the country are starting to see the benefits this type of arrangement offers, so more of these jobs are becoming available. What's difficult is finding an inbound telemarketing job at a call center that pays a salary plus commissions.

"Inbound telemarketing requires the same basic skills as outbound telemarketing, but the personality traits needed to be successful with inbound telemarketing are slightly different, because there's much less frustration and rejection. I believe outbound telemarketing is far more challenging than inbound telemarketing. In terms of dealing with objections, inbound telemarketers have many of the same challenges as outbound telemarketers. Some of the common objections relate to money or the need to check with a spouse before making a purchase.

"When someone is looking for an inbound telemarketing job, in addition to the standard benefits offered to all full-time employees, they should consider the work environment, the work schedule, and the bonuses or perks being offered as part of the compensation package. There is a wide range of inbound telemarketing opportunities out there, not just at call centers, but at medium- and large-sized businesses and corporations as well. The biggest perk we offer to our top performers is the ability to work from home. Not everyone wants to work from home, however. Some people choose to work in order to get out of their house. It's important to find an environment you'll be comfortable working in."

Q. How do you keep your telemarketers motivated and keep them from getting bored repeating the same scripts over and over?

A. "I have found that offering a wide range of different contests and incentives throughout each day and during each week helps a lot. The fact that our telemarketers are earning a commission on their sales also boosts motivation dramatically. I have supervisors monitor calls to insure someone's attitude and performance is at the right level. We also use an outside training company that comes in periodically and offers training and motivation to our employees. A lot has to do with building up the belief our telemarketers have. They need to believe in the product and have certain beliefs about the customers they're dealing with. We do motivational training every two weeks in order to encourage the right attitude and the right level of enthusiasm. I also encourage my employees to use other common tricks to keep morale up. For example, we place mirrors on everyone's desk so they can see themselves work. Finally, choose an employer that will give you the technological tools, the necessary training, and the ongoing support to help you make sales."

Conclusion

PREPARE TO KICK OFF YOUR TELEMARKETING EFFORTS

Well, there you have it: the telemarketing techniques you need in order to achieve success as a telephone sales professional. What's required now is the investment of time and energy on your part to do the necessary research and work to properly implement what you've learned. Of course, as with any new set of skills, mastering them will require plenty of practice. Don't be afraid to spend time rehearsing your sales pitch before making calls. Consider your selling ability to be a set of skills that will evolve and grow over time, allowing you to achieve even greater success.

The great thing about telemarketing is that your ability to make a sale has little to do with the state of the economy or what's happening in the world around you. Consumers and companies alike will always have a need for products and services that can help solve a problem or benefit them in some way. By identifying the appropriate prospects and educating them about the products/services you're offering, you will make sales. It all starts by picking up the telephone!

Appendix A

KNOW THE LAWS—
BEFORE YOU PICK UP
THE TELEPHONE

A s you read this section, keep in mind the following:

- This section was created to provide general information only and should not be considered legal advice (after all, I am not a lawyer).
- State and local laws relating to telemarketing vary greatly. Thus, you should consult with your own attorney.
- There are many additional laws and guidelines pertaining to telemarketing that have not been discussed in this section.

Especially when it comes to cold calling consumers at their homes, there are laws in place designed to protect people from unwanted calls. As a telemarketer, it's important to have a basic understanding of the federal as well as related state laws. Since the passage of the 1991 Telephone Consumer Protection Act, state telemarketing laws and regulations have increased, and they continue to evolve. Each state has implemented unique regulations, exemptions, and penalties addressing such issues as registration, caller identification, and statewide or telemarketer-specific do not call lists. In January 2002, 25 states introduced new legislation intended to further regulate telemarketing practices.

The Federal Trade Commission ((202) 382–4357/ *www.ftc.gov*) defines telemarketing as "a plan, program, or campaign which is conducted to induce the purchase of goods or services by use of one or more telephones and which involves more than one interstate telephone call. The term does not include the solicitation of sales through the mailing of a catalog which: contains a written description or illustration of the goods or services offered for sale; includes the business address of the seller; includes multiple pages of written material or illustrations; and has been issued not less frequently than once a year, when the person making the solicitation does not solicit customers by telephone but only receives calls initiated by customers in response to the catalog and during those calls takes orders only without further solicitation. For purposes of the previous sentence, the term 'further solicitation' does not include providing the customer with information about, or attempting to sell, any other item included in the same catalog which prompted the customer's call or in a substantially similar catalog."

Under the federal regulations, one of the restrictions put upon telemarketers is the time calls may be made to consumers. Although some individual state laws may be more restrictive, the federal law states, "Without the prior consent of a person, it is an abusive telemarketing act or practice and a violation of this Rule for a telemarketer to engage in outbound telephone calls to a person's residence at any time other than between 8 a.m. and 9 p.m. local time at the called person's location."

During a call, the telemarketer *must* disclose specific information, including the identity of the seller, that the purpose of the call is to sell goods or services, the nature of the goods or services, and that no purchase or payment is necessary to be able to win a prize or participate in a prize promotion if a prize promotion is offered. This disclosure must be made before or in conjunction with the description of the prize to the person called. If requested by that person, the telemarketer must disclose the no-purchase/no-payment entry method for the prize promotion.

Although the laws themselves use a significant amount of legal terminology in their wording, the Federal Trade Commission summarizes additional national telemarketing laws as follows:

- It's illegal for a telemarketer to call a prospect if he or she asked not to be called (or has put himself or herself on a "do not call" list).

- It's illegal for telemarketers to misrepresent any information, including facts about their goods or services, earnings potential, profitability, risk or liquidity of an investment, or the nature of a prize in a prize-promotion scheme.

- Telemarketers must tell the prospect the total cost of the products or services they're offering and any restrictions on getting or using them, or that a sale is final or nonrefundable, before the prospect pays. In a prize promotion, the telemarketer must tell the prospect the odds of winning, that no purchase or payment is necessary to win, and any additional restrictions or conditions of receiving the prize.

- It's illegal for a telemarketer to withdraw money from a prospect's checking account without his or her expressed, verifiable authorization.

- Telemarketers cannot lie to get a prospect to pay, no matter what method of payment will be used.

Additional free information about the national laws pertaining to telemarketing is available from the Federal Trade Commission's Website. Point your Web browser to *www.ftc.gov/bcp/rulemaking/tsr/index.html.*

To develop a full understanding of the local and national telemarketing laws, you can subscribe to *Telemarketing Regulations & Compliance Procedures 2002*, published by the Securities Industry Association (*www.sia.com*; $595 annual subscription). This is an easy-to-understand guide to all state telemarketing regulations and compliance procedures, plus a summary of federal telemarketing rules and regulations. A paid subscription to this service includes access to SIA's Telemarketing Publications Web page, featuring an electronic version of the annual publication, plus access to a regularly updated section on introduced legislation and future trends.

Appendix B

DON'T GET CAUGHT UP IN TELEMARKETING FRAUD

very year, consumers lose more than $40 billion by fall-
ing victim to telemarketing fraud. Over the years, criminals have perfected the use of the telephone to engage
in fraudulent activities. According to The U.S. Department of
Justice (*www.usdoj.gov*), "Telemarketing fraud is a term that
refers generally to any scheme to defraud in which the persons
carrying out the scheme use the telephone as their primary
means of communicating with prospective victims and trying to
persuade them to send money to the scheme. When it solicits
people to buy goods and services, to invest money, or to donate
funds to charitable causes, a fraudulent telemarketing fraud
operation typically uses numerous false and misleading statements, representations, and promises."

Assuming you represent a legitimate company using
telemarketing as part of your normal business practices, it is
important to understand how and why others are using the telephone for illegal purposes. The U.S. Department of Justice
reports that even legitimate businesses can get caught up in
fraudulent schemes, possibly through a practice referred to as
"reloading," where criminals could contact your customers or
prospects without you knowing about it.

"Reloading is a term that refers to the fraudulent telemarketer's practice of recontacting victims, after their initial transactions with the telemarketer, and soliciting them for additional payments. In prize-promotion schemes, for example, victims are often told that they are now eligible for even higher levels and values of prizes, for which they must pay additional (nonexistent) 'fees' or 'taxes.' Because reload transactions typically demand increasingly substantial amounts of money from victims, they provide fraudulent telemarketers with their most substantial profits, while causing consumers increasingly large losses that they will never recoup voluntarily from the fraudulent telemarketers," reports the Department of Justice.

Statistics show that at any given time, there are hundreds of fraudulent telemarketing schemes being perpetrated on consumers in the United States. Where do these fraudulent telemarketers obtain their leads? Well, just as legitimate telemarketers do, they routinely buy leads from legitimate lead brokers. As a result, the person you may be calling for as part of your telemarketing effort may have recently received a call from someone trying to commit fraud against them, which means you must overcome even stronger negative feelings the prospect may have about telemarketers.

The Federal Trade Commission reports that some of the most common telemarketing scams include:

- Charities: Criminals often invent charities for which they use fraudulent telemarketing practices to raise money.

- Investments: Every year, ordinary (and well-educated) people lose millions of dollars as a result of falling for fraudulent investment schemes sold to them over the telephone. Some of the common investments sold in these schemes include gemstones, rare coins, oil and gas leases, precious metals, art, and other investment opportunities.

- Prize Offers: The person receiving the call typically needs to do something in order to get the free prize, such as attend a sales presentation, buy something, or for some reason disclose his or her credit card information. In these situations, the prize(s) offered are generally worthless or drastically overpriced.

- Recovery Scams: Once a consumer falls for a telemarketing scam, yet another scam is used to solicit a service that will help the victim recover his or her lost money (for a fee, of course).

- Travel Packages: Free or drastically discounted vacations are promoted, but in reality, these vacations can wind up costing a bundle, or the trips never actually take place.

- Magazine Subscription Sales/Renewals: Prospects are "sold" subscriptions to nonexistent magazines or legitimate magazines that never actually get processed or filled, because the fraudulent telemarketer has no affiliation with the magazine and keeps the money.

- Vitamins and Other Health Products: Various sales pitches are used to sell products at extremely high prices that are worth very little. These and other schemes tend to be targeted to senior citizens.

Appendix C

MAKE SURE YOUR LEGITIMATE PITCH DOESN'T SOUND LIKE A SCAM

The Federal Trade Commission offers the following tips to consumers to help them identify when they're being targeted in a fraudulent telemarketing scheme. As a legitimate telemarketer, make an effort to insure your sales pitch won't be misconstrued as fraudulent by your prospects.

The FTC reports that some of the common strategies used during fraudulent telemarketing activities include:

- Telling the prospect that he or she must act now or the offer won't be good, or that he or she can't afford to miss out on this "high-profit, no-risk" offer.

- Telling the prospect that he or she has won a free gift, vacation, or prize, but he or she must pay for "postage and handling" or other charges to obtain the prize.

- Informing the prospect that he or she must send money, give a credit card or bank account number, or have a check picked up by courier before being given a chance to consider the offer carefully.

- Telling the prospect that he or she does not need to check out the company with anyone, such as a family member, lawyer, accountant, the local Better Business Bureau, or any consumer-protection agency. Some bogus justification will be offered to substantiate this.

- Implying that the prospect does not need any written information about the company or references.

Fraudulent telemarketers continue to help ruin the reputation of legitimate telesales professionals. In many cases, this means you'll need to work even harder to build trust quickly between you and your prospects.

INDEX

ABOUT
THE AUTHOR

Ellen Bendremer (*www.EllenBendremer.com*) is an accomplished sales and telemarketing professional with more than 15 years' experience in her field. In 1991, she founded The Innovations Group, Inc., a company dedicated to providing training, motivational speaking, and consulting to businesses looking to enhance the skills and effectiveness of their sales force. She is known for her innovative approach to increasing sales performance by utilizing telemarketing techniques and applications. Ellen resides outside of Boston with her family.